Bags for Fashic

FRO͏ ON

VP

nani coldine

Bags for Fashionistas

designing * sewing * selling

nani coldine

Schiffer Publishing Ltd®

4880 Lower Valley Road • Atglen, PA 19310

Other Schiffer Books on Related Subjects:

A Century of Handbags, Kate Dooner, 978-0-8874-0465-8

A Passion for Purses: 1600–2005, Paula Higgins & Lori Blaser, 978-0-7643-2617-2

Published by Schiffer Publishing, Ltd.

4880 Lower Valley Road

Atglen, PA 19310

Phone: (610) 593-1777; Fax: (610) 593-2002

E-mail: Info@schifferbooks.com

For our complete selection of fine books on this and related subjects, please visit our website at www.schiffer-books.com. You may also write for a free catalog.

This book may be purchased from the publisher. Please try your bookstore first.

We are always looking for people to write books on new and related subjects. If you have an idea for a book, please contact us at proposals@schifferbooks.com.

Schiffer Publishing's titles are available at special discounts for bulk purchases for sales promotions or premiums. Special editions, including personalized covers, corporate imprints, and excerpts can be created in large quantities for special needs. For more information, contact the publisher.

Photographs: Yvonne Sieler

Originally published as Taschen für Fashionistas by Haupt Verlag, © 2011 Haupt Berne. Translated from German by Jonee Tiedemann.

Copyright © 2015 by Schiffer Publishing

Library of Congress Control Number: 2015943719

ISBN: 978-0-7643-4912-6

Printed in China

About the author

Nadine Kulis is the designer and illustrator behind the name nani coldine. After completing her fashion studies in London and Antwerp, she founded the handbag label nani coldine and created a design company of the same name. Her handbags have been published in *InStyle* and *Elle* and are sold all over the world. After many years of producing her bags in several countries, she now manufactures her limited editions in Germany. Nadine and her team also provide many fashion companies with bag designs and ideas. Her love of the craft and her passion for unusual and creative designs and bags are still her main source of motivation. With *Bags for Fashionistas*, she proves that making things yourself is not only rewarding but also chic.

Nadine Kulis currently lives and works in Cologne, Germany. She writes her own bag blog: www.bagstage.info. More information about nani coldine can be found here: www.nanicoldine.com.

nani coldine

The team around nani coldine consists of a network of creative fashionistas. The following people have participated in this project:

Yvonne Sieler: photos, graphics, and layout

Verena Zerwas: model, graphics, and layout

Evelyn Breuers and Angela Sophia Marques: models and trainees for design assistant, model development, illustration, research, design layout, and pattern development.

Many thanks to Julia Becker Ritterspach for the photo on the XXL print tote, Johanna Lambsfuß for the background reports for this book at www.bagstage.info, and

Reyhan Yildirim for the drawings on pages 22 and 23.

CONTENTS

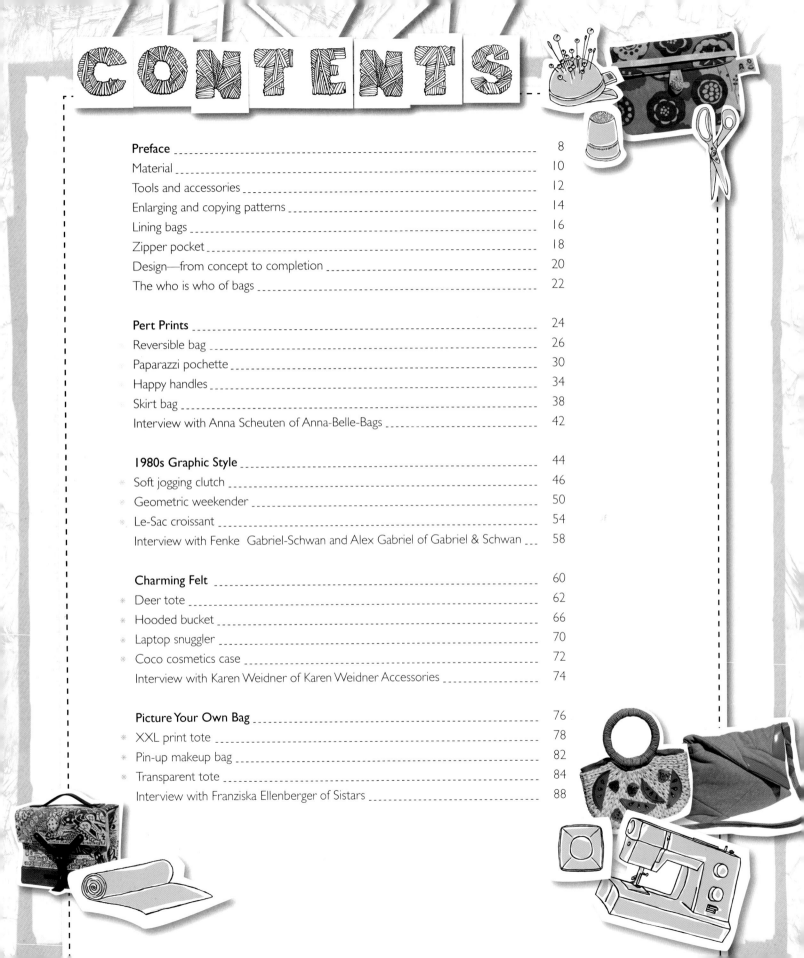

Preface

The indispensable bag

Is there any woman who is not crazy about handbags? No accessory, scarf, belt, or even a pair of Manolos can provide a woman with more glamour and personality more quickly than the right bag.

The mysterious cachet of the handbag contrasts J22 with its pragmatic function as a form of transporting items. A bag contains one secret or another and yet cannot keep anything to itself. With one glance into a woman's bag, you get a quick psychogram: receipts with telephone numbers, chewing gum, overdue traffic tickets, lipsticks and their lost caps, and even emergency ballerina buns. The daily handbag is a close confidante in all situations of life. However, it should not only match your outfit but also express your style.

But what to do in times of economic uncertainty and design overload? Which bag matches my style for the coming spring season? Do I have to spend a small fortune yet again to call a unique bag my own? Good news, the answer is: no!

Why handmade?

Do-it-yourself (DIY) is a trend that not only saves money but allows you to match items to your specific needs, to be independent from brands, and, most important, to enjoy the gratification of developing your own idea, executing it, and showing it off.

In an era of mass consumption, the personal and handmade has special value. This book will provide countless ideas and instructions for making your own dream model. So rather than taking out your credit card, let your fantasy run wild. You will have twice the fun.

The second pillar

The online marketplace presents many possibilities for sharing your creations with the world. Creative people use blogs and forums to exchange ideas and opinions, and the multitude of sales platforms on the Internet are slowly but surely democratizing the market. Even if you have no desire to convert your talent into money, it is interesting to contemplate the possibilities. Apart from the joy of making things, many creative types ask themselves: how can I create a second pillar, or, how can I best sell my collection? This is why we will cover the commercial side of handbag-making. In addition, you will find interviews with successful handbag designers.

Requirements

Designers usually complete several years of training, while tailors do an apprenticeship. This book is no replacement for such training. However, in order to make the bags in this book, you should have a basic understanding of sewing and know how to use a sewing machine. (If you need a refresher course, consider enrolling in a local sewing class.) If you can't find the manual of your dusty sewing machine, simply download it from the Internet.

The instructions for our bags are detailed and every step is well-illustrated. Each model features a logo marking its difficulty:

(👜 beginner, 👜 👜 hobby sewers, 👜 👜 👜 advanced). Even novices, however, will find inspiration for jazzing up old bags in the Pimp My Bag chapter, simply by using a hot glue gun, accessories from the sewing box, and grandma's button collection. If you don't like to study instructions or are impatient, let our models inspire you, and modify them to your heart's desire.

Let's get started!

On these following pages, we are delighted to show you how to create fashionable designs with simple means and basic experience. So relax and have fun. Once you have learned to develop your own designs, you will have a different perspective on the ready-made products that surround you. And if your first piece has a few skewed seams, remember:

Perfection is boring—small errors are charming!

MATERIAL

The fabrics from which bag dreams are made are quite varied.
Many types are perfect for making bags.

Terrycloth towels

Flock

Linen

Fabrics

Sturdy fabrics

Because bags are used daily, designers prefer robust materials such as felt, awning fabric, linen, canvas, wool blankets, leather, artificial leather, imitation animal prints such as repile patterns, fur and faux fur, and jacquard or decorative fabric.

Recycled fabrics

Why always buy new when you can reuse items:
Army surplus blankets and tents, swimming caps, leather jackets, truck awnings, umbrellas, old tape cassettes, plastic tablecloths, bicycle tubes, jeans, and terrycloth towels.

Delicate fabrics

Fine materials are popular for evening bags:
satin, velvet, lace.

Upgrades

Add a personal touch to existing bags with:

Appliqués, decorations, and color

You can jazz up boring bags using needle and thread, brush and pen, or a hot glue gun. Try using buttons and pearls, embroidered motifs, spangles, rivets, bands, braids, trim, feathers, fabric and leather flowers, diamond motifs, draperies, smock details, batik or fabric painting, thick felt pen, or acrylic color.

Prints

Have you ever thought about printing your bag? Even if you don't plan to start a large production, there are plenty of techniques for individual pieces. Consider screen prints, flock prints, foil transfer prints, stencil prints, fabric for inkjet printers, and digital prints.

Handles and straps

Handles and bags should match. Sturdy straps are practical to carry over your shoulder. Ready-made handles and rings lend an elegant and high-quality appearance.

Ready-made handles and straps
Double handles in U-shape (standard), oval double handles, bamboo rings

Alternative handles and straps
Leather belts, chains (from the hardware store), nylon straps, cords, ropes and jump ropes, seatbelts, and handmade handles sewn to desired length. Scraps from pant and skirt waistbands are perfect for making handles and straps.

Handles

Straps

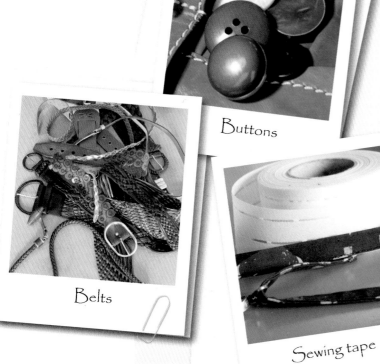

Buttons

Belts

Sewing tape

Inserts

Inserts give a bag more strength and can be as thick or thin as the bag requires. Consider inserting interfacing, cotton batting, or even fabric scraps. Sewing tape is a good choice for bulking up handles and straps.

Fasteners

Your belongings should be secure while they are being transported. Think about zippers, buttons, and Velcro®.

Tools and Accessories

This section lists the essential tools you will need to make your bag.

Workbench and cutting table
Prepare a space where you can cut the patterns and fabrics (okay, it could be on the floor, too).

Pattern paper
You can buy classic pattern paper already printed with a grid. It works well for enlarging the design patterns in this book.

Pencil and eraser
Quite obvious, don't you think?

Triangular ruler or cutting ruler
Indispensable for marking seam allowances and right angles, or to modify the pattern.

Scissors
Apart from a good pair of fabric scissors, you should also invest in paper scissors and perhaps a pair of pinking shears.

Tailor's chalk
Mark the outlines of the paper design patterns on the back of the fabric.

Scissors can be sharpened by cutting fine sandpaper.

Tip

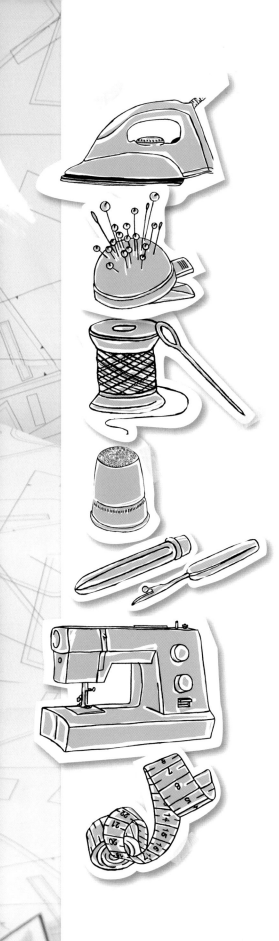

Iron and ironing board

A steam iron is ideal. It will be your trusted colleague, from cutting the pattern to closing the very last seam. Before and between the different steps it is all about ironing, ironing, ironing.

Pins and pincushion

We prefer long, stainless steel pins with large, colored heads that are easy to see in the fabric. With your pincushion on your wrist, you always have your little helpers handy.

Needle and thread

Make sure that the type of needle matches the fabric. This is particularly important for sewing machine needles. Check the gauge and purchase special needles for jeans, leather, and stretch fabrics. The same is true for threads and yarns. Choose the right gauge, tearproof quality, and, most important, the right color!

Thimble

It protects your perfectly painted fingernails from nasty pricks and stings.

Seam ripper

Don't be discouraged if you sew something the wrong way. That's where the seam ripper and some patience are indispensable.

Sewing machine

If you haven't used your sewing machine for some time, you should probably read the manual again (if you lost it, download it from the Internet) and try out some stitches and seams on scrap fabric.

Measuring tape

The flexible measuring tape, hanging nicely around your neck, helps you check for consistent lines and seam allowances.

Mise en place!

Just as you would in the culinary arts, we suggest you lay out your tools and materials on your workbench before beginning a project.

Enlarging and Copying Patterns

With a few exceptions, a pattern accompanies each bag in this book. But before you pick your favorite one, roll out fabric, and cut it to size, familiarize yourself with the basic principles of our pattern system.

The materials lists correspond exactly to the bag model presented. You are welcome to make modifications. If you decide to enlarge the pattern, you will need more material.

The dart marks the line where the fabric is sewn.

The red triangles mark the places where the fabric is folded.

Almost all of the pattern sections include a seam allowance of ½-inch. Pay attention when you enlarge the patterns, as some pattern sections (handles, insert bottoms, and loops) are indicated with larger seam allowances, or even without them.

Pattern explanation: here you find a list of all the pattern sections of a given model as well as how many pieces have to be cut from the material.

Markings are helpful to align the pattern sections before sewing.

The arrow indicates the grain of the fabric.

The fold line indicates the edge where the fabric is folded.

One square of the design pattern grid equals 2 x 2 inches.

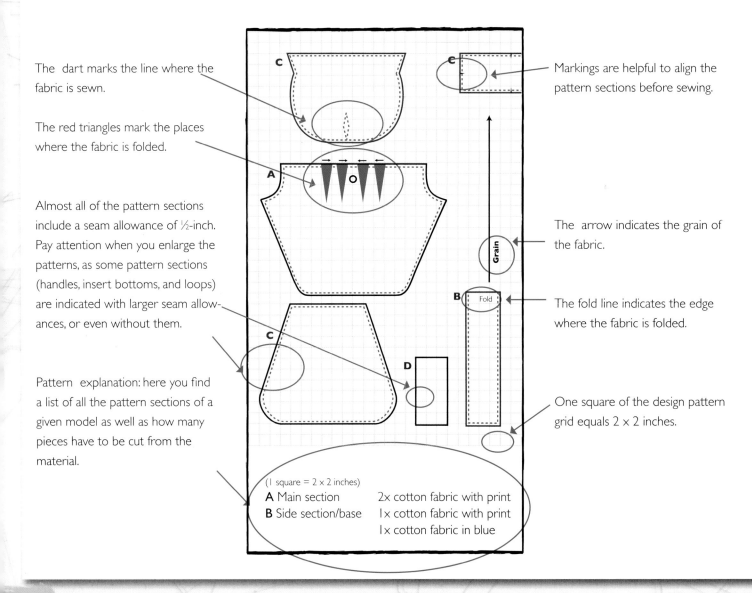

(1 square = 2 x 2 inches)
A Main section   2x cotton fabric with print
B Side section/base   1x cotton fabric with print
                                     1x cotton fabric in blue

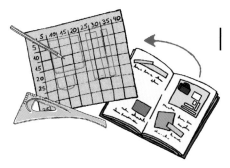

I Enlarging and transferring

Using grid paper available at art supply stores, you can enlarge our patterns 1:5 and transfer them onto pattern paper. Draw all of the darts and markings.

Darts or markings

To transfer darts or other markings onto several layers of fabric, use a long thread with loose stitches to hold the layers in place. Cut the loose loops and carefully remove the pattern paper.

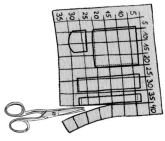

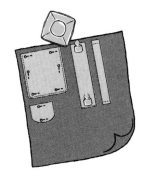

2 Cutting out

Now carefully cut out the design patterns. Make sure you pay attention to how many times each section needs to be cut.

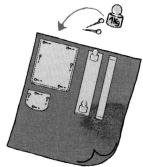

3 Pinning

Carefully pin the patterns to the back of the fabric or use weights to position them.

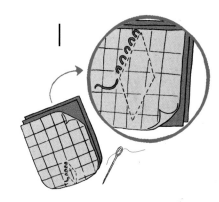

I

4 Tracing

Then trace the outline of the patterns on the fabric with tailor's chalk. Do the same with darts and markings.

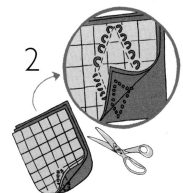

2

5 Cutting

Now you can cut the fabric.

Lining Bags

With a few exceptions, this book includes instructions for the matching lining. However, if you want to incorporate nifty details such as inner compartments, feel free to improvise.

Patch Pocket

1 First, measure the largest items that will need to fit in the pocket: width × length × height.

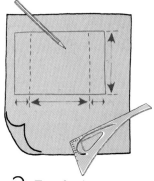

2 Transfer the measurements onto pattern paper.

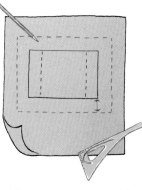

3 Add some space around this basic shape, about 1¼ inches, as well as a seam allowance of ½-inch, or 1½ inches all around.

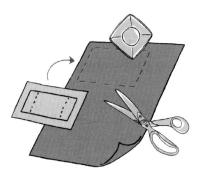

4 Transfer the completed piece onto the fabric with chalk and cut it out.

5 Fold the upper and lower edge under ½-inch twice and topstitch.

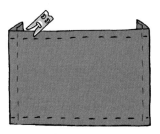

6 Repeat with the side seams.

7   Stitch the finished pocket onto the fabric.

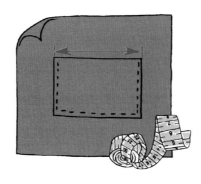

8   You can also add a flap. Measure the width of the pocket first.

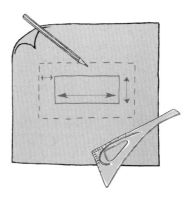

9   On pattern paper, draw a rectangle in the dimensions you want and add a seam allowance of ¾-inch all around.

10   Now transfer the outline to the fabric with chalk and cut it out.

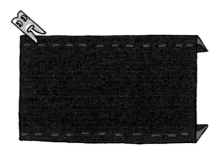

11   Fold the upper and lower edge under ½-inch twice and topstich.

12   Repeat with the side seams.

13   With right sides together, place the flap onto the fabric about ½-inch from the pocket top. Stitch along the lower edge.

14   Fold down the flap, iron, and stitch.

Tip

You can also sew on the inner pockets from the outside.

Zipper Pocket

Now that you have learned how to create your own pocket design, we will show you how to increase your capabilities: a hidden zipper pocket is ideal for guarding your treasures from thieves.

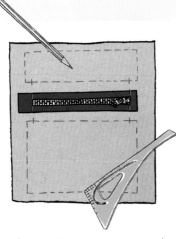

1 To make a pattern, measure your chosen zipper. Add ½-inch to each end of the length and make two rectangles from them (a 6-inch zipper would result in 7-inch-long rectangles).

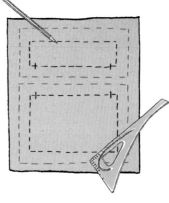

2 Add a seam allowance of 1½ inches around the rectangles.

3 Transfer the patterns onto fabric with chalk and cut them out.

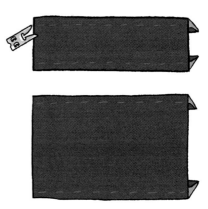

4 Fold the upper and lower edges under ½-inch twice and stitch.

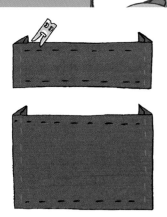

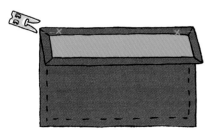

5 Repeat with the side seams.

6 Place the pocket sections with right sides together, pinning the outer edges at the beginning and end of the zipper. The zipper will be inserted in the middle section that remains open.

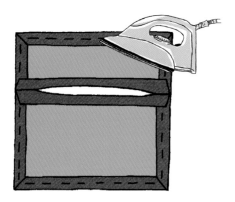

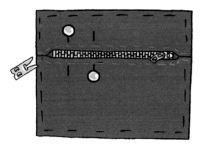

7 Iron the seam allowance.

8 Place the zipper onto the pocket from the back and stitch on the right side.

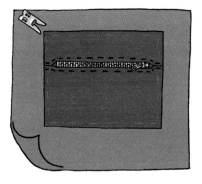

9 Place the finished pocket where you want it and sew. Done.

Design—from Concept to Completion

Of course you could dive right into making your favorite model in this book. However, if you prefer a more conceptual approach to designing models and collections, follow these design tips.

1. Research

A search for materials, colors, and decorations should be the starting point of your first creations. A casual find at a garage sale or in the attic could be the basis for an entire collection. Included here are plenty of suggestions for materials. It is up to you to find the best combinations for your bag.

2. Mood board

Professional designers use a mood board to develop an overview of materials, colors, and other items they collect. Arrange whatever inspires you on a pinboard or bulletin board—scraps of fabric, photos, newspaper clippings—until your ideas harmonize and a concept begins to take shape.

3. Sketchbook

Keep your sketchbook handy. Make it a habit to sketch out interesting details of everyday life, paste some scraps, and take notes. Use the sketchbook to collect ideas, fabrics, and sketches. It documents your progress, from the first scattered ideas to the design specifics.

4. Design sketches

Now you can convert your collected ideas into the first designs. If your initial sketches were rough, work out the details now. The more precise your idea on paper, the easier it will be to execute—more so if you require help from others. Think about the side and back of your design. If you can't draw well, use collages or trace complex details with carbon or tracing paper.

Use the models in this book as a source of inspiration. Think of the designs as a modular system that allows you to combine your favorite details into new variations.

If you are not yet ready to make your own bag design, simply start with a square model or use a pattern from the book that comes closest to it. This is the base on which any number of modifications can be made. You can change the size and proportions while laying out the body of the bag, including details like the style of the handles. You'll find design pattern basics on page 14.

5. Selecting materials

You will choose materials at the same time you are working on the design, as the two should match. Check your mood board regularly to see how far you are veering from your original idea. Before cutting, do a few tests with your sewing machine to see how the chosen material responds and how it can be worked. You should have a clear idea about whether your model will be soft and pliable or firm and stiff. Take note of other details like colors and the size of decorative bands, zippers, and lining while compiling your materials.

7. Test run

It's a good idea to make a test model from scraps. This allows you to check whether the three-dimensional object matches your concept, particularly regarding size. Put the model on your shoulder and look at it in front of a mirror, or ask another person to model it. Mark or pin corrections on the test model. Transfer the corrections onto the pattern. To be really confident about the result, make a final test model.

6. Pattern development

Before you start developing a pattern, make a precise sketch of the model, including the front, rear, and sides. The more detailed your idea, the more fully the design pattern can be realized.

8. Finale

When you are convinced that the materials and proportions are right, you are ready to make your bag.

The  of bags

The *weekender bag:* jet-setting

type: unisex bag
application: airplane, train, business meeting

As the name suggests, the weekender bag is perfect for things you need for a weekend. Fitted with many cool inner compartments, it has become the first choice of women who like to be on the move but don't want to use a backpack or trolley suitcase. But it is not limited to jet-setters; everyone appreciates a stylish bag for the weekend trip. Aside from travel use, it's also perfect for running from one appointment to the next. It is large enough to hold a large water bottle, several pieces of clothing, a laptop, camera, and cellphone, and of course cosmetics.

The *tote bag:* the activist

type: city shopper
application: supermarket, park, demonstrations

The *tote bag* is available in many variations, from the simple cotton bag from the supermarket to the richly decorated Gucci babushka tote. This style is currently trendy because it is simple and ecological and signals political correctness.

About thirty years ago the tote bag found its way into the world of fashion. Back then it started out as the accessory of ecologically minded people and as a "cloth-instead-of-plastic" item that addressed environmental issues and promoted fair trade. When it became fashionable to go green, the tote was adopted as a handbag alternative. Designers interpreted the bag using new materials and noble leathers, with handles just long enough to sling it around your arm.

But what, exactly, distinguishes a handbag from a stylish tote? The difference is only in the mind of the wearer. The tote bag not only reminds others of the issues at hand, it draws attention to the owner. The tote signals authenticity and credibility.

The *hobo bag:* bohemian princess

type: pouch bag
application: art exhibit, philosopher's café, Alanis Morissette concert

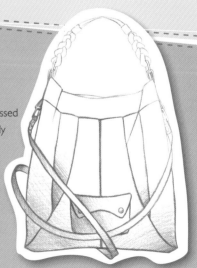

With its crescent shape and long handles, the hobo bag is usually carried over the shoulders or crossed over the back (now quite fashionable). It comes in all colors, particularly in earth tones, and is usually made from soft material like leather or cotton. It is crumply by nature, which expresses a bohemian vibe—the hobo is boho. The look is usually adopted by women with intellectual and artistic tendencies and those who like to disregard what is currently trendy. So if you prefer an alternative hippie style and like to wear long, flowing skirts, embroidered tunics, belts with large buckles, and embroidered boots, just add the hobo bag and you will be all set.

The *clutch:* evening beauty

type: evening bag
application: gala, party, opera, fine restaurant

The term clutch is fairly self-evident—that's what you do with it. The small diva among the handbags, with its average size of 9 inches x 5 inches, looks more like an XXL wallet. So, you hold it under your arm or in your hand. It sounds awkward, but the woman wearing such a gem will radiate irresistible glamour; it has nothing to do with being comfy! Over the years, the clutch has been fine-tuned with ever more glamorous variations. Anything and everything has been used: pearl embroidery, bows, crystals, feathers, and the finest materials like crocodile leather and mink. Actually, the clutch is regarded as a low-key accessory that should not distract from the main attraction: the elegant lady and the beautiful evening. This compact carrier is reserved for VIP content like lipstick, a credit card, and a cellphone.

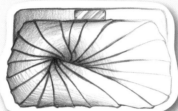

The *baguette bag:* bag and the city

type: city shopper
application: café, club, first date

This longish model was the ultimate bag shape during the late 1990s, when Fendi reinterpreted its baguette from the 1920s and Sarah Jessica Parker featured it in the cult television series *Sex and the City.* The baguette can be tucked under the arm, just like the French do with their bread. However, it is more flexible than the clutch because of its handles, which are just long enough to sling it over the shoulder.

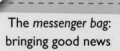

The *pochette:* mini all-arounder

type: evening bag
application: after-work party, carry inside a larger bag

This French term **pochette** means cover, bag, decorative cloth, or envelope. It is a convenient, flat, and elegant woman's handbag similar to the previously described clutch and offers the wearer about as much space. Because of its cuddly form it is easy to carry inside a larger bag. In contrast to the clutch, the pochette has handles in order to be worn over the shoulder. Once you come to appreciate this bag, you will understand why it is really an all-rounder.

So, ladies, if you are about to pack your weekender for your next trip, use your pochette as your cosmetics container. Once you empty its content in the sink of the hotel, you have the perfect evening bag for the restaurant and night club.

The *messenger bag:* bringing good news

type: unisex bag
application: at the turntable, college, coffee shop, on the bike

Known as a postman's bag, shoulder bag, or DJ bag, this sporty model for everyday use is straighforward, just like its owner, perhaps. It is popular with school kids, students, and still-young professionals who need their energy for things other than carrying stuff around, and it allows for easy, hands-free transport.

This model, often preferred by men, is based on the classic postman bag. It features a large flap and a long, sturdy, adjustable strap. This bag is often made from robust and washable materials and even recycled industrial materials. The Swiss Freitag brothers managed to land this bag big-time in the late 1990s when they made messenger bags from truck awning fabric.

Pert Prints

Bags are like clothing: a nice fabric with a cool print is all it takes! Consider decorative fabrics commonly used for other purposes. How about terrycloth, canvas, or those colorful window curtains? Interior design fabrics usually have a sturdiness that works quite well for handbags.

paparazzi pochette

happy handles

reversible bag

skirt bag

Reversible Bag

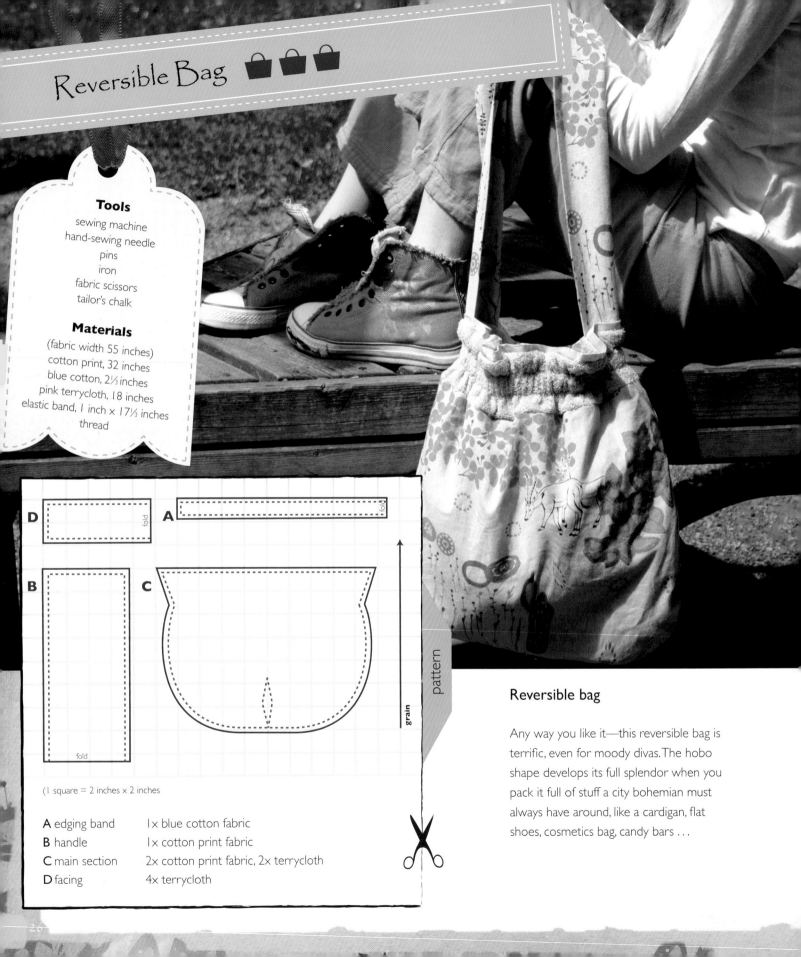

Tools

sewing machine
hand-sewing needle
pins
iron
fabric scissors
tailor's chalk

Materials

(fabric width 55 inches)
cotton print, 32 inches
blue cotton, 2⅓ inches
pink terrycloth, 18 inches
elastic band, 1 inch × 17⅓ inches
thread

D A fold

B C

fold

(1 square = 2 inches × 2 inches)

grain

pattern

A edging band   1× blue cotton fabric
B handle   1× cotton print fabric
C main section   2× cotton print fabric, 2× terrycloth
D facing   4× terrycloth

Reversible bag

Any way you like it—this reversible bag is terrific, even for moody divas. The hobo shape develops its full splendor when you pack it full of stuff a city bohemian must always have around, like a cardigan, flat shoes, cosmetics bag, candy bars . . .

1 Enlarge and transfer the pattern sections, and cut as indicated. Also transfer the rhombic-shaped dart on section C.

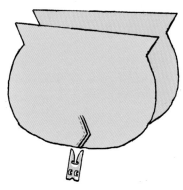

2 Sew the darts on the terrycloth and cotton print fabrics.

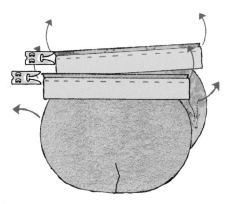

3 Stitch the facing pieces D onto the four main sections C, right sides together, along the top edge. Iron apart the seams so they lay flat.

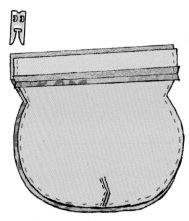

4 Sew together the outer pockets, right sides together.

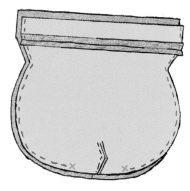

5 For the inner pocket, sew the terrycloth, right sides together, and leave a 6-inch opening in the lower center.

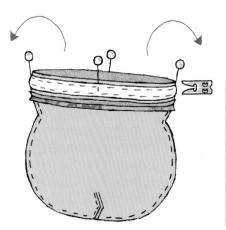

6 Sew the elastic band ends together along the short side. So that it can be sewn onto the facing of the outer bag, fasten the stretched band at four points and sew together. Then turn the bag inside-out.

Tip

While sewing, stretch the elastic band in sections from pin to pin. Beginners might want to use more pins to hold it steady.

27

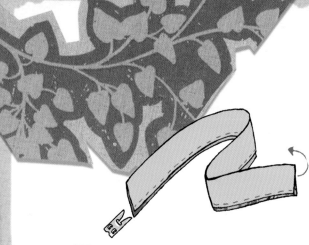

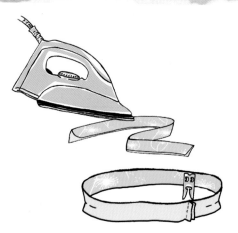

7 Sew the handles together lengthwise, right sides together, turn inside-out, and iron.

8 Fold the edging band lengthwise, iron, and open again. Join the ends and iron apart the seam.

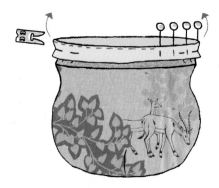

9 Sew the edging band, right sides together, onto the facing of the main section.

10 Using a narrow seam, sew the handles over the side seams on both sides of the outer bag.

11 Now place the outer bag into the lining bag.

12 Sew the edging band to the lining bag. Sew the two seam allowances of the edging band together.

13 Now turn the bag inside-out through the opening in the lining fabric.

14 Match the facing. On the right side, topstitch two parallel seams onto the elastic band.

15 Close the opening in the terrycloth by hand using blind stitches. Iron the narrow edging band once more so it lays flat.

16 Done.

outside/turned inside-out

voilà

29

Paparazzi Pochette

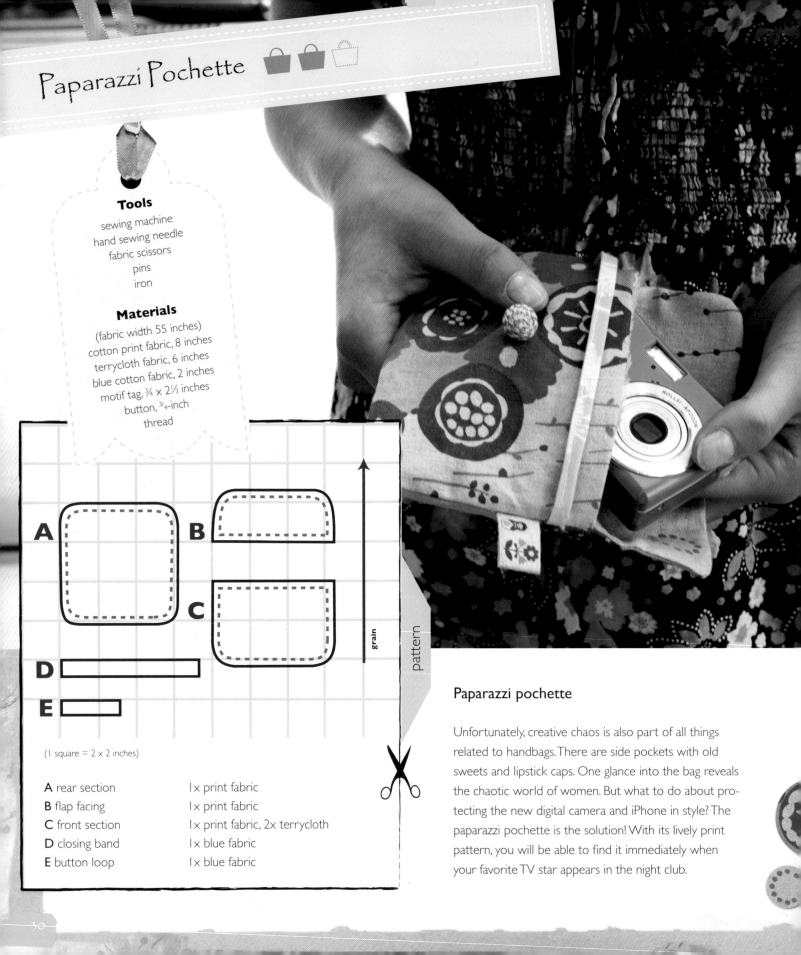

Tools

sewing machine
hand sewing needle
fabric scissors
pins
iron

Materials

(fabric width 55 inches)
cotton print fabric, 8 inches
terrycloth fabric, 6 inches
blue cotton fabric, 2 inches
motif tag, ¾ × 2⅓ inches
button, ¾-inch
thread

A **B**

C

D

E

grain

pattern

(1 square = 2 × 2 inches)

A rear section	1× print fabric
B flap facing	1× print fabric
C front section	1× print fabric, 2x terrycloth
D closing band	1× blue fabric
E button loop	1× blue fabric

Paparazzi pochette

Unfortunately, creative chaos is also part of all things related to handbags. There are side pockets with old sweets and lipstick caps. One glance into the bag reveals the chaotic world of women. But what to do about protecting the new digital camera and iPhone in style? The paparazzi pochette is the solution! With its lively print pattern, you will be able to find it immediately when your favorite TV star appears in the night club.

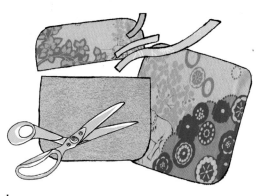

1 | Enlarge the sections and cut them as indicated.

2 | Fold the closing band in half, iron, and fold each edge under ¼-inch. Iron and narrowly stitch.

3 | Place this band 1 inch from the upper edge onto the right side of section C and sew onto both sides. Place the motif tag slightly under it and sew into the seam allowance.

4 | Now sew the outer pocket, right sides together. Stop ½-inch from the top edge of section C and turn the bag inside-out.

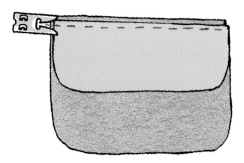

5 | For the lining, sew together facing B and a terrycloth section C. Iron the seam.

6 | Now place the two terrycloth sections C with right sides together and close the sides. Stop ½-inch from the top edge. Leave an opening of about 2 inches at the lower center.

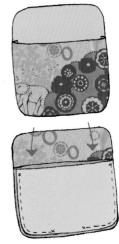

7 With right sides together, place the outer pocket into the inner pocket.

8 Sew together the front edge from the inside and the outer pocket from seam to seam.

9 Make the loop for the button just like the closing band (step 2) and insert it between the lining and the outer pocket.

10 Sew facing B onto the outer pocket from seam to seam. When closing the sides, make sure that the seam aligns perfectly at the front side.

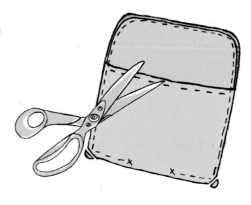

11 Trim the corners and round areas.

12 Pull the bag through the opening onto its right side.

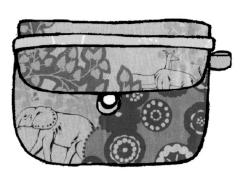

13 Close the opening in the lining by hand with blind stitches or the sewing machine.

14 Sew the button onto the front pocket.

voilà

Apropos paparazzi

Heathrow Airport 2006: scandal girl Lindsay Lohan leaves her favorite orange Birkin bag on her trolley and five minutes later the bag has disappeared, including its contents: jewels worth about $1 million. The poor girl freaks out when she notices the theft and promises a finder's fee. The bag was found in the airport garage; however, the finder's fee was never paid.

By the way ...

Happy Handles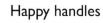

Tools

sewing machine, sewing needle
iron
fabric scissors
paper scissors
double-sided adhesive tape
tailor's chalk, pins

Materials

(fabric width 55 inches)
cotton print fabric, 43 inches
blue cotton fabric, 40 inches
2 wooden or cardboard rings, 7½ inches
facing band, about 40 inches per handle of
7½-inch-diameter
2 snap hooks, 2 D-rings
sewing tape, 43 inches
cardboard or stiff interfacing, 6 × 12 inches
magnetic closure, ¾-inch
thread

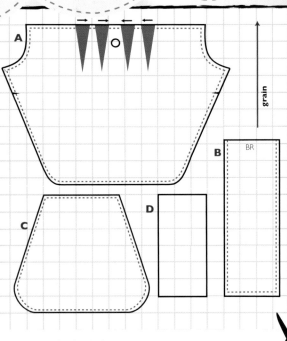

(1 square = 2 × 2 inches)

A	main section	2× cotton print fabric
B	side section/base	1× cotton print fabric
		1× blue cotton fabric
C	lining section	2× blue cotton fabric
D	base	1× cardboard/interfaceing

Happy handles

Handles can be a real eye-catcher and impart special character. In this case we have simply wrapped bands around two cardboard circles. The band choice is up to you, but it should match the color of the bag material. We have also added a long strap so you can wear it the way you like best.

1 Enlarge and transfer the patterns and cut as indicated. Transfer the folds of sections A and the markings for the magnetic closure.

2 Make the fabric folds of the A sections, folding toward the inside at the markings.

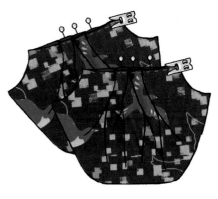

3 Pin the folds and baste to hold them in place.

4 Sew on the magnetic clasps.

5 Sew or iron the cardboard or interface D, onto the center of B (left side).

6 Now add the facing band to the outer seam of the front and back sections. This lends a polished look and provides more firmness at the edges.

7 Sew the front and back pieces of the pocket onto the side piece B. Sew only up to the markings on the sides of section A. Stop sewing ½-inch from the end of section B (seam allowance). Now turn it around onto the right side.

8 Flip the upper lateral tips outward—both edges, or the entire curve. Sew together and turn right-side-out.

 Tip

You can add extra-long straps to other bags that have short handles. This lends a more casual look if you wear it across the body.

9 If you have not yet done so, get some old wooden handles or cut two rings from thick cardboard (about 7½ inches in diameter). Put double-sided tape on the handles and wrap the handle with an edging band or other attractive fabric. Secure the end with a few stitches.

10 Now pull the tips of the bag from the outside to the inside through the handles and sew them to the layer of fabric below. Careful: the seam should not be visible from the outside; sew carefully by hand.

11 For the long strap, cut a strip of 3-inch x 43-inch printed cotton fabric and iron onto the sewing tape. Cut two 2⅔-inch-long loops from them.

12 Fold the strap and the loops and sew along the edge.

13 Stitch from the inside of both D-ring loops to the upper edge of the side pieces.

14 Now sew the pieces of lining fabric together.

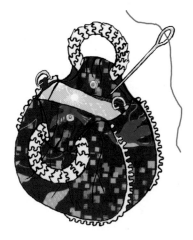

15 Place the lining bag into the outer bag.

16 Sew in the lining by hand: the blind stitch is the cleanest; iron ½-inch of seam allowance toward the inside first. Professionals may try this with the sewing machine.

17 Thread the long straps into the snap hook and stitch. Place the straps on the bag. Done.

voilà

Skirt bag

This striking bag was inspired by a woman's go-to garment: the skirt. The beautifully printed and colorful cotton fabric is gathered into a band that resembles a slender waist. To take it a bit further, we added matching trim and a ready-made handle. It is easy to make, even for beginners.

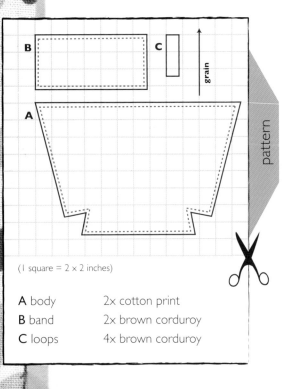

(1 square = 2 × 2 inches)

A body   2x cotton print
B band   2x brown corduroy
C loops   4x brown corduroy

grain

pattern

Tools

sewing machine
pins
iron
fabric scissors
paper scissors

Material

(fabric width 55 inches)
cotton print fabric, 18 inches
brown corduroy, 8 inches
striped trim, 1¼ × 32 inches
red zigzag trim, 28 inches
thread

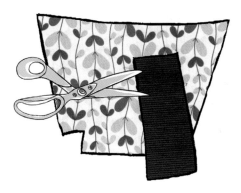

| Enlarge and transfer the patterns and cut as indicated.

2 Cut the zigzag edging in half; cut 14 inches from the striped edging and put it onto the lower third of one of the facing sections B.

3 Make a loop with 15¾ inches of the striped trim and fasten it to the corduroy band. Use the remaining trim to make a loop; tack it to the left side of the band.

4 Baste the bag sections by hand, or with the sewing machine using the largest possible stitch.

5 Gather the fabric to 12½ inches wide.

6 Sew the band sections, right sides together, to the upper edge of the front and rear gathered sections.

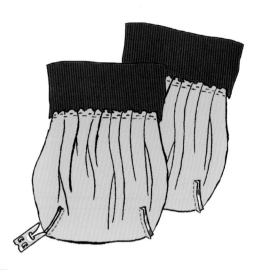

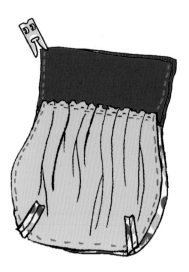

7 Sew the darts at the front and rear sections and iron them apart. Flip the facing up.

8 Sew together front and rear sections of the bag, right sides together, and turn it around, inside-out.

9 Flip half of the facing to the inside, pin, and stitch from the outside as invisibly as possible.

10 Sew four loops from the corduroy. Match the width of the loops to the width of the handle opening, fold with a seam allowance of ¾-inch, and sew together.

Printing fabrics

A beautiful print turns a fabric into an eye-catcher. People have printed fabrics for thousands of years using wooden stamps that made it possible to repeat patterns and motifs. Later, industrial textile printing revolutionized the craft. Even today, however, despite the use of digital processes, the success of a fabric print depends on the creativity and skill of the designer.

By the way . . .

Tip

Sew the loops from the inside so the seam remains invisible.

| | Put the loops around the handle eyelets and sew from the inside so it remains invisible.

12 Done.

Tip

The fabrics, bands, and handles in this chapter were provided by www.frautulpe.de

voilà

with Anna Scheuten, founder of *Anna-Belle-Bags*

Anna Scheuten
Mühlenkamp 18
40229 Düsseldorf
www.anna-belle-bags.de
info@anna-belle-bags.de

Anna Scheuten, the founder of Anna-Belle Bags, has been fascinated by bags since early childhood. She created her first pieces while studying fashion design and discovered that it was a lot of fun. But she knew that it would be difficult to compete in the fashion industry as a no-name and without start-up capital. Nevertheless, she wanted to give it a try, thinking that reasonably priced retail offerings for stylish, unique bags and accessories were limited, as the bags made by major brands were prohibitively expensive. This is how, in 2006, the idea developed for a proprietary label with its own production and online distribution. The highlights of the collection were, and still are, the revolver bags, which fortunately have not caused any problems when the owner steps into a bank.

How did it all begin?

For a long time I had had the idea for a revolver bag collection. As a student, I liked to go to parties, and I needed a practical, cool-looking bag that I could wear while dancing. I created design patterns and then began making bags for friends and family, and finally I put together my own collection. The trick is to let your clients choose among the different models, leather colors, and fittings to customize their bag.

Where can we see your bags, and how much do they cost?

The distribution is mainly online, but we also work with retail shops in Germany, Austria, and on Ibiza. The bags range from roughly 59 to 299 euros ($64 to $326), depending on the model, material, and size.

We use mainly lambskin, high-quality grained and embossed artificial leather, and some unique fabrics. The bags are one-of-a-kind designs and materials, as opposed to the cheap products from Asia and the Far East. We also like to use rivets, edging, braids, and fringe for a typical Ibiza hippie look.

Who are your customers?

Men and women of all ages and from all walks of life who value quality and individuality and are prepared to pay for it. Our customers are people who like to be trendsetters; they are open-minded, have a good sense of humor, and are life-affirming. This includes not only customers in Germany but also neighboring countries such Austria, Switzerland, Great Britain, France, Spain, the Netherlands, and Belgium.

What is your favorite bag from your current collection?

That would be *Joline* in yellow (top right).

Do you manufacture your own bags or contract them out for production? What should beginners know about producing their own series?

The bags are fabricated only after the order is received, so they are made locally in Germany. Sometimes we offer limited editions, which are usually made in advance. But the bags are enjoying a lot of popularity now, so we wouldn't rule out series production in the future. I would like to keep production in Germany to create jobs in this country. If we were to mass-produce our bags, we would be careful to maintain the individuality and exclusivity.

You are running a large online shop on your website. What is the role of the Internet as a distribution channel? What other distribution networks are you working with, such as retailers?

The online shop is our main distribution channel. This way we get not only regional customers, but business from other countries, as well. It is common for retailers and other agencies to notice our products, and we have established some partnerships, including distribution via other online portals, such as www.dawanda.com.

Anna Belle

1980s Graphic Style

As a fashionista, you know that the 1980s are back, and you are adept at incorporating these second-hand finds into your wardrobe. If stone-washed jeans, leggings, shoulder pads, and neon orange wallpaper come to mind, don't worry: we have sifted through the bloopers of good taste and present only the best of this revival: graphic appliqués, re-interpreted for today.

Soft jogging clutch

Geometric weekender

Le-Sac croissant

Tools

sewing machine
fabric scissors
tailor's chalk
iron
hand sewing needle
pins

Materials

(fabric width 55 inches)
gray cotton jersey, 47 inches
pink patent leather, 2¾ inches
sewing tape, 45 inches
wadding, 41 inches
pink thread

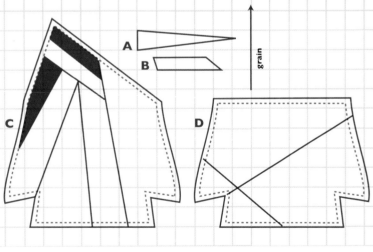

(1 square = 2 x 2 inches)

A	appliqué	1x pink patent leather
B	appliqué	1x pink patent leather
C	main section with flap	2x cotton jersey, 1x wadding
D	front/rear liner	2x cotton jersey, 1x wadding

Soft jogging clutch

Ever since the sportswear craze of the 1980s, designers have been pondering a dilemma, and customers are standing in the shops, clueless. They are all looking for that one definitive mix of sporty and elegant. It has to be chic, but it shouldn't be too stiff. Our gray soft jogging clutch made from cotton jersey combines those features. It is soft and fluffy without much ado or an elaborate interior.

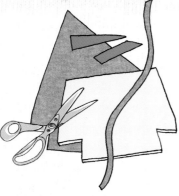

1 Enlarge and transfer the patterns and cut as indicated.

2 Place the wadding insert onto the jersey sections and narrowly stitch.

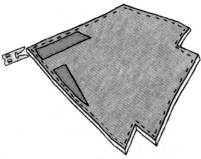

3 Topstitch the two geometric patent leather forms (as you like, or as shown in the pattern here).

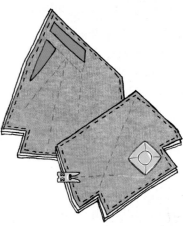

4 Transfer the stitch markings and topstitch with pink thread. The wadding lends a quilted effect.

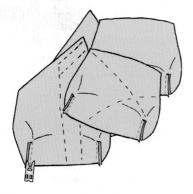

5 Sew the edge darts on the outer pockets and sew the lining darts.

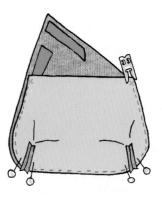

6 Sew together the outer bag with a ½-inch seam allowance. Stop about ½-inch from the upper edge of the bag and turn right-side-out.

Tip

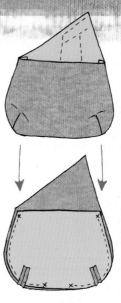

7 Repeat step 6 on the lining bag, but leave a
4-inch opening at the lower center.

8 Put the outer bag into the inner bag.

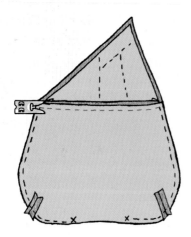

9 Sew the inner and outer bags together along
the upper edge.

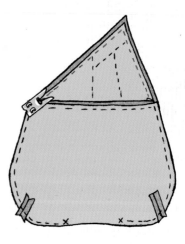

10 Now sew the bag flap.

11 Pull inside-out through the opening.

12 Close the opening in the lining with a blind
stitch or sewing machine.

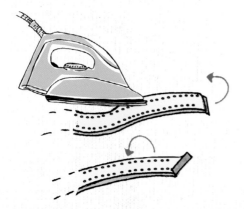

14 Topstitch the handle lengthwise.

13 Cut a handle from the jersey, making a strip 3 × 45 inches and iron onto the tape. First fold the short sides ½-inch and then the long sides as shown in the diagram.

16 Sew the handle to the outer edges.

15 Topstitch the small patent leather shapes.

By the way ...

About jogging pants

Pop stars like the Spice Girls and Eminem wore athletic pants during their concerts, despite the negative image. When you are jumping around on stage, oversized sport clothes are comfortable. But the clothing also became a fashion statement Elsewhere, sports classics from the 1970s gained a somewhat ironic cult status.

voilà

Geometric Weekender

Tools

sewing machine
leather needle if required
fabric scissors
pins
tailor's chalk
iron

Materials

(fabric width of 55 inches)
synthetic dark-brown suede leather,
32 inches
synthetic gold leather, 8 inches
ironing insert, 32 inches
sewing tape, 107 inches
zipper, 28 inches
edging, ½ x 28 inches
thread

grain

pattern

(1 square = 2 x 2 inches)

A main section left	2x imitation suede, 2x insert
B main section right	2x imitation suede, 2x insert
C bottom	1x imitation suede, 1x insert
D top side section	2x imitation suede, 2x insert
E side section	2x imitation suede, 2x insert
F handle	4x imitation suede

Geometric weekender

This roomy weekender was inspired by polygon shapes and tangram puzzle motifs. Finally—a bag most men will also appreciate. This weekender is a welcome change to the usual travel bag, and it pretty much guarantees that you will get to chat with a charming co-traveler.

1 Enlarge and transfer the pattern markings and cut as indicated.

2 Iron the matching inserts onto all the sections to achieve the required firmness.

3 Cut out geometric forms from the gold synthetic leather and stitch onto the front of the two sections (A+B).

4 Iron the four handle sections onto sewing tape (each 27 inches long), folding the edges where indicated, and topstitch the two handles.

5 Sew the two parts (A+B) of the front and rear section.

6 Topstitch with matching or contrasting thread.

Sew a lining for this bag if you like. Simply transfer the pattern onto lining fabric, follow the instructions, place one bag inside the other, and blind stitch by hand. Another option is to cover the inner seams with colored bias tape.

Tip

7 Mark the position of the handles on the front and rear sides with tailor's chalk and sew the handles crosswise.

8 Sew the zipper between the two upper side pieces D.

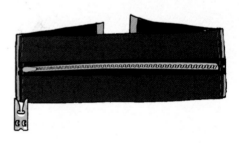

9 Optional: topstitch a band onto the shorter side E.

10 Sew the side sections E on each end of the closed zipper.

About men's bags

The man's handbag phenomenon appeared during the 1970s in the form of a leather briefcase with a sling. What caused this trend? The film *Saturday Night Fever* made tight, sexy clothing fashionable for men, and there simply was no place to carry things in your pockets. But the bag fell out of favor in the 1980s and disappeared from the male wrist. Despite the efforts of noted designers, the bag never saw a revival, and men have been stuffing things into their pants pockets ever since.

By the way . . .

Tip

Tip

Reinforce the bottom with cardboard or extra-thick inserts. Shorten section C all around ½-inch and transfer onto cardboard.

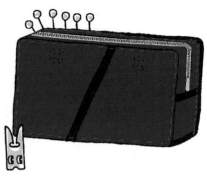

11 Sew this section (zipper with side pieces) to the bottom C. This creates circular sides.

12 Now sew the side section between the front and back of the weekender. Make sure you observe the markings, smooth out the fabric, and pin it in many places before sewing.

13 Done!

voila

Le-Sac Croissant

Le-Sac croissant

First we explained what a baguette is (the who is who of bags) and now we present you with a croissant. Okay, the important thing is that they are crunchy and delicious! We are not Fendi's grandchildren, but this bag looks quite a bit like the It Bag! With its bold patches and your favorite old belt, this elegant bag can be tucked under the arm or worn casually across the body.

Tools
sewing machine
leather needle, if required
fabric scissors
tailor's chalk
pins

Materials
(fabric width 55 inches)
patterned decorative fabric, 18 inches
caramel synthetic leather, 10 inches
gold synthetic leather, 10 inches
lining fabric, 25½ inches
2 eyelets, 1½ inches
belt
thread

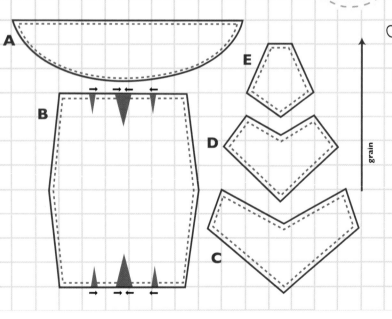

pattern

grain

(1 square = 2 × 2 inches)

A upper end   2x decorative fabric, 2x lining fabric
B center section   1x decorative fabric, 1x lining fabric
C side section   2x caramel synthetic leather, 2x lining fabric
D side section   2x gold synthetic leather, 2x lining fabric
E side section   2x caramel synthetic leather, 2x lining fabric

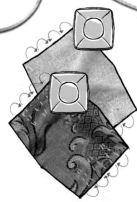

1 Enlarge and transfer the patterns and cut as indicated. Transfer the folds onto section B.

2 Mark the folds with tailor's chalk on the B sections (decorative and lining fabric). The following steps also apply to the lining fabric sections.

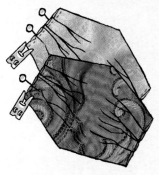

3 Place the folds onto the B sections and stitch along the upper edge.

4 Sew center section B to side section C, working carefully at the edges.

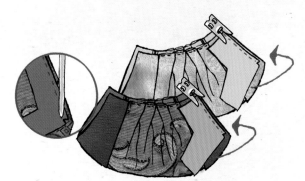

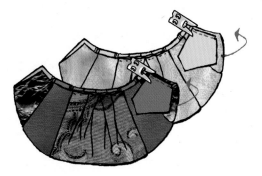

5 Sew side section D to section C.

6 Sew section E to side section D.

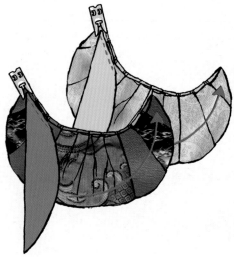

7 Sew the crescent-shaped section A to the resulting curve.

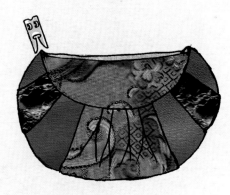

8 Topstitch on the right side so it lies flat.

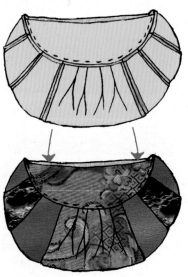

9 Place the lining bag into the outer bag.

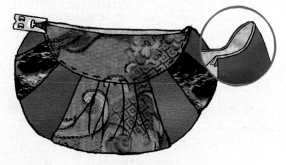

10 Fold the seam allowances at the upper edge of the bag toward the inside between the lining and the outer bag (iron first) and stitch the circumference.

Tip

Large eyelets are available at curtain retailers. For the best results, take your bag to an interior designer, who will have the appropriate tools.

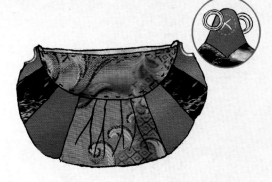

| | Insert the eyelets on each side.

| 2 Use an old belt as a handle. Thread it through the eyelets and close the buckle.

| 3 Done.

Tip

As an alternative to a belt and eyelets, sew a strap from fabric and iron it onto sewing tape. Then sew it to the ends of the bag between the outer fabric and the inner lining.

voilà

with Fenke Gabriel-Schwan and Alex Gabriel of *Gabriel & Schwan*

Alex Gabriel & Fenke Schwan Gbr
Zossener Straße 51
10961 Berlin
www.gabriel-schwan.de
mail@gabriel-schwan.de

Fenke Gabriel-Schwan and Alex Gabriel are domestic as well as business partners and founded the accessory brand *Gabriel & Schwan* after graduating from their product-design studies. Their education covered not only the design of furniture and home accessories but also bags, shoes, and jewelry. Their first collection grew out of their student projects. When they moved from Cologne to Berlin in 2010, they discovered that Berlin was a better place to get noticed as a German fashion brand. The city offers young designers abundant options for workplaces and networking.

Do you have a role model or a continuing source of inspiration?

A few Scandinavian fashion labels target a similar market as we do. We look at what they are doing to find new retailers and examples of development. Friends and art are always an important source of inspiration, too.

Where do you sell your creations, and how much do they cost?

We exhibit our products at various events. Several retailers represent our products, none of them in Germany. The bags and accessories are priced between 45 and 160 Euros ($50 and $175) .

What is your favorite piece or the best-selling item from your current collection?

The bestseller from the current collection is the knotted chain, followed closely by *Le Sac midi* (top right).

We noticed that you are listed in large online shops like Etsy and Dawanda, and you also run your own online business. Do you view the online shop as a viable alternative to a brick-and-mortar store?

For us, online sales are simply a way to offer our products directly and to lower stock volume. We are in personal contact with the customer. But it is not an alternative to a real store.

What are the best fashion shows to participate in?

The fashion festival *WeddingDress* is one of the sales events we like best. It is held once a year during Fashion Week in Berlin in summer, and it is one of the best-attended events.

Where is your manufacturing done?

At the moment we are still making everything in our own studio, but if our orders get larger, we would like to have the production done in eastern Germany.

From hobby to career, how long do you think it takes for a new label to establish itself?

This would be different in each case and depends mainly on the designer's financial means. It can take five to seven years to establish yourself.

What advice do you have for beginners?

When we started out, we called on various shops to find new clients. Often we only had a few photos of our bags. Some of the shop owners were very open, but many times we were not taken seriously. Today I would do things differently. I'd suggest making a first contact by phone or email. Present yourself as professionally as possible, from production photos to your website and flyers. Once we had improved these things, our sales went much better. Other people take you as seriously as you take yourself.

Gabriel & Schwan

Charming Felt

Felt is a humble material that doesn't get the respect it deserves. The soft, dense material is easy to work with, and it comes in gorgeous colors. Add appliqués and embellishments, and you have a handbag that's chic and sleek. Here we present four spectacular models ready for you to make them a reality. They combine felt's understated charm with a nifty pink deer, colorful twirled brooches, and woven slogans.

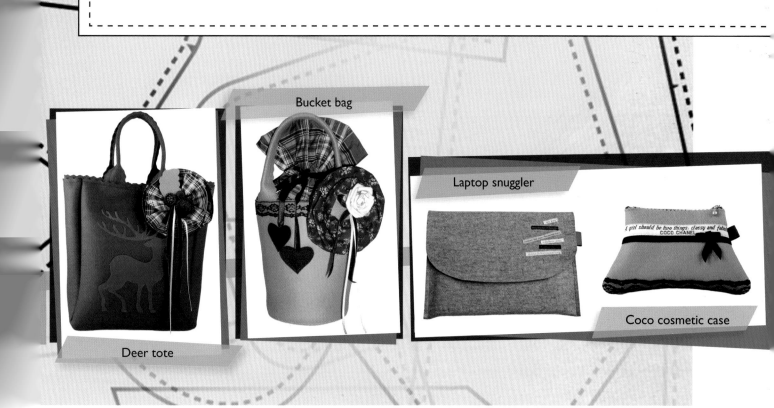

Deer tote

Bucket bag

Laptop snuggler

Coco cosmetic case

Deer Tote

Tools

fabric scissors
pinking shears
iron
pins
computer

Materials

(fabric width 55 inches)
olive felt, 20 inches
pink felt, 2½ inches
checkered cotton fabric, 20 inches
corded ribbon, 1 × 40 inches
perhaps a pushbutton, ¾-inch
flock-printed deer motif

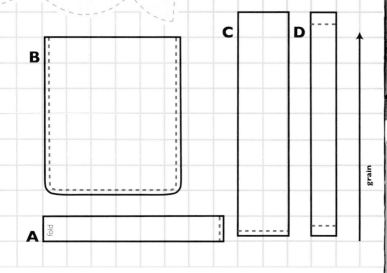

B

C D

grain

A fold

(1 square = 2 × 2 inches)

pattern

A lining   1× olive felt
B main section   2× olive felt, 2× checkered cotton fabic
C side section   2× olive felt, 2× checkered cotton fabric
D handle   2× olive felt

Deer tote

What to wear to the next outdoor festival?
With this deer on your arm, you can let out
your inner Heidi.

1   Enlarge and transfer the sections and cut as indicated. Cut the handle with pinking shears.

2   Trim the upper edge of the front, back, and side sections with pinking shears.

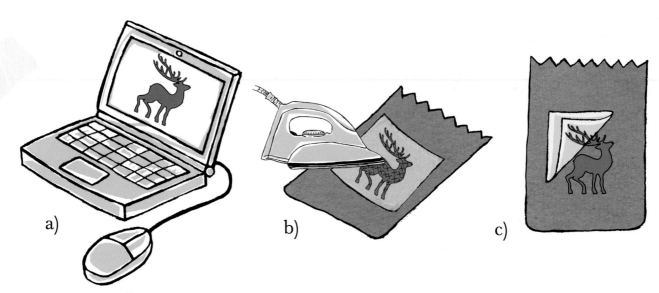

a)   b)   c)

3   The motif: Trace the deer on page 123. You can use any motif you like, ideally converted to a digital graphic. Many copy shops offer flock printing.

Simply email the graphic to a copy shop with a plotter, which creates the motif. Iron the motif onto the front of section B as indicated and let cool. Remove the foil.

4 Now sew together the outer bag and lining bag. Sew side pieces C between the front and rear sections. Sew along the pinked upper edge to finish in a clean line, and sew each side from the top down. Careful! Use plenty of pins before you start sewing.

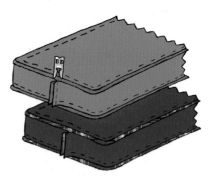

5 Sew together the side sections, meeting at the bottom center. Repeat with the lining sections.

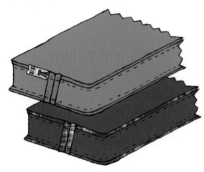

6 Flatten the seams and close the small opening.

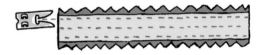

7 Stitch the corded band with three parallel seams onto the wrong side of the felt handle.

8 Sew together the center section of the handle. This way it lies better in your hands.

9 Make a circle with the pink trim and sew the ends together. Fold the seams apart and stitch.

Tip

We recommend magnetic metal buttons for closing the bag.

10 Now topstitch the lining bag, right sides together, to the pink trim so that it lies over the lining when you look into the finished bag. If you wish, you can now insert a pair of magnetic buttons into the front and rear sides, centered in the trim.

11 Position the handles on the inside at the same height and fasten them with pins. Then place the trimmed lining into the bag. If you work with a contrasting color as shown here, let the trim stick out about ½-inch at the top.

12 Sew the lining onto the outer bag and the handle.

By the way ...

An opulent brooch provides the finishing touch. See the instructions on page 120.

13 Done.

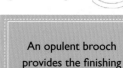

voilà

Hooded Bucket

Hooded bucket

The little bucket is the perfect container for a spontaneous picnic with your summer love. It will easily hold two small sodas with a straw and a clutch of fresh fruit. With this accessory on the picnic cloth, you can dip your manicured toes into the lake and feed your loved one sweet strawberries.

Tools

sewing machine
hand sewing needle
fabric scissors
paper scissors
hot glue gun
iron
pins
safety pin
pinking shears

Materials

(fabric width 55 inches)
green felt, 20 inches
checkered cotton fabric, 20 inches
red felt, 4 inches
lace, 1 × 27 inches
satin band, ½ × 36 inches
cardboard, 6 × 6 inches
thread

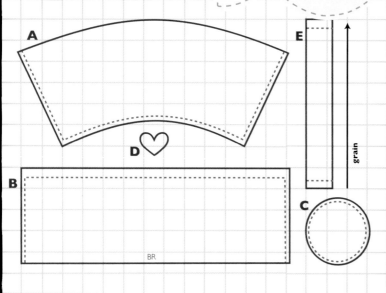

(1 square = 2 × 2 inches)

A outer wall	1× green felt	
B hood	1× checkered cotton fabric	
C bottom	2× green felt, 1× cardboard	
D heart	2× green felt, 2× red felt	
E handle	2× green felt	

pattern

66

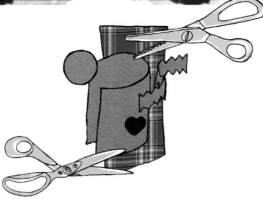

1 Enlarge and transfer the patterns and cut as indicated. Cut the handles with the pinking shears.

2 Sew together the outer wall A at the side and carefully turn around to the right side.

Sewing the bottom with the sewing machine is tricky. If necessary, sew by hand.

Tip

3 Fold the seam allowances apart and topstitch so they lie flat.

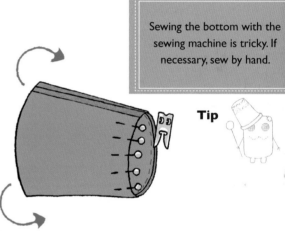

4 Sew the felt bottom to the outer wall. First pin the bottom well so the curve is even, stitch, and turn around to the right side.

5 Topstitch around the bottom of the bucket for definition and firmness.

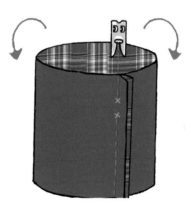

6 Sew together hood B along the short side. Leave a roughly ¾-inch space at the lower third for the drawstring. Flip the upper half to the outside so the right side faces out.

7 Stitch a ¾-inch-wide tunnel for the satin draw-string (step 6). The ends of the satin band will emerge from the open section. Finish the lower, open edge of the hood with a zigzag stitch.

8 Stitch the corded band with three parallel seams onto the felt handles.

Tip

Our model gets a charming touch with an added brooch. You can find the instructions on page 120.

9 Now stitch the center section of the handle together. This will cause it to lie nicely in your hands.

10 Sew the handles parallel to each other from the inside of the bag.

11 Place the hood ¾-inch into the bucket and sew from the outside. Then insert the cardboard bottom and put the second felt bottom on top of it. Fasten with a few drops from the hot glue gun so it fits tightly.

12 Sew the lace onto the upper edge of the bag, all the way around. This helps to reinforce the hood and handles. Thread the satin band through the drawstring tunnel with a safety pin or large sewing needle.

voilà

13 Pin the ends of the satin bands to a red heart and sew together.

You can buy special computer paper that lets you print out a slogan and then iron the text onto your fabric. Another option is to embroider the quotes by hand or with your sewing machine.

Tools

sewing machine
fabric scissors
pins

Materials

(fabric width 55 inches)
gray felt, 18 inches
band, 1 × 3 inches
velcro tape, ¾ by × 4 inches
slogans, ½ × 4 inches
thread

A

(1 square = 2 × 2 inches)

grain

pattern

A   main section   1× gray felt

Laptop snuggler

So you're working from a home office? With high-speed Wi-Fi connections, there's no reason not to sit in a coffee shop on the street corner. And the laptop needs a secure container, decorated with cool slogans so the people at the next table know who they're dealing with.

By the way ...

Our pattern is perfect for the Mac-Book Pro®. Simply adjust the size to your laptop.

1 Download slogans from the Web or choose other appliqués such as a flock motif like our deer model on page 62. Then your purse and laptop snuggler will be a set.

2 Enlarge and transfer the pattern and cut out as indicated. Transfer the markings for the flap, Velcro, and band.

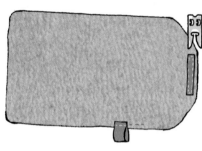

3 Topstitch the rough side of the Velcro band to the left side of the flap at its center, ½-inch from the edge. Form the short band into a loop and stitch it to the side, about 10 inches from the top edge.

4 Place the slogans onto the flap and stitch. Stitch the other half of the Velcro band about 6 inches from the lower edge of the bag, on the right side of the fabric.

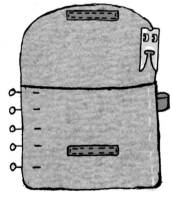

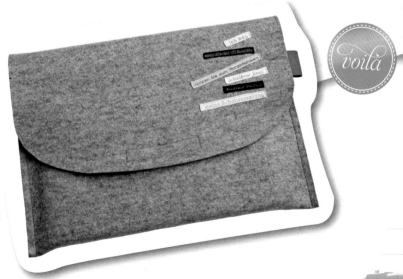

voilà

5 Flip the lower section upwards at its marking (10 inches). Pin the side seams and close them.

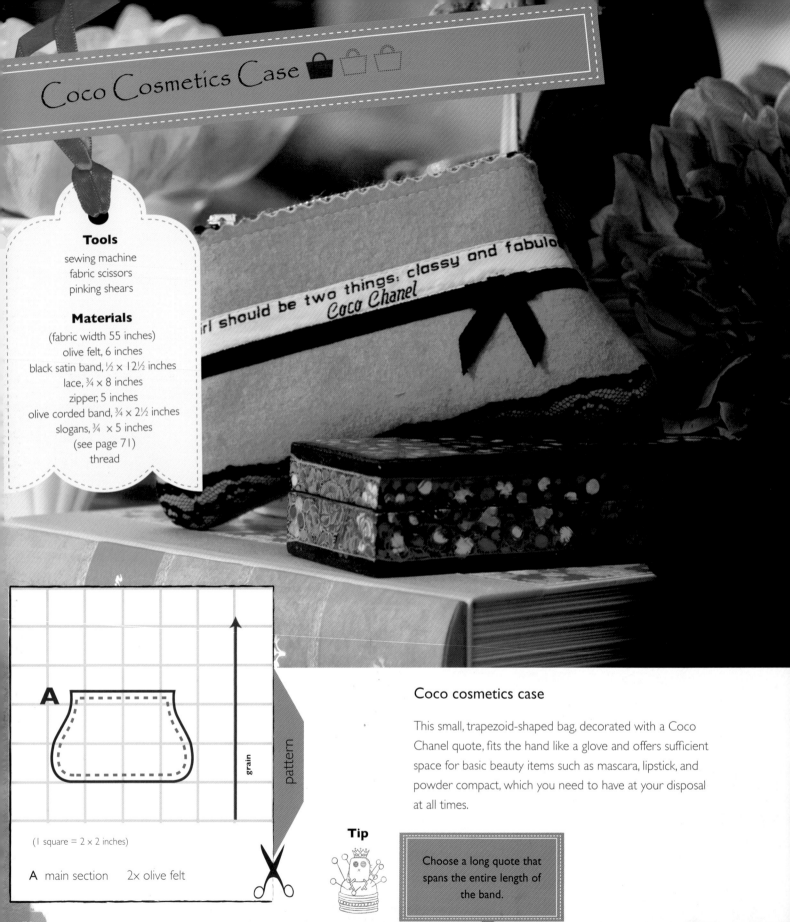

Coco Cosmetics Case

Tools

sewing machine
fabric scissors
pinking shears

Materials

(fabric width 55 inches)
olive felt, 6 inches
black satin band, ½ × 12½ inches
lace, ¾ × 8 inches
zipper, 5 inches
olive corded band, ¾ × 2½ inches
slogans, ¾ × 5 inches
(see page 71)
thread

A

grain

pattern

(1 square = 2 × 2 inches)

A main section   2x olive felt

Coco cosmetics case

This small, trapezoid-shaped bag, decorated with a Coco Chanel quote, fits the hand like a glove and offers sufficient space for basic beauty items such as mascara, lipstick, and powder compact, which you need to have at your disposal at all times.

Tip

Choose a long quote that spans the entire length of the band.

1 Enlarge and transfer the pattern and cut indicated.

2 Trim the top edge of the bag with pinking shears.

3 Cut off 6 inches from the satin band and make a bow. Stitch the remaining satin band, bow, slogan, and lace onto the front.

4 Make a loop from the corded band and fasten it to the front side, facing inward, with a few stitches.

5 Place the zipper between the front and back sections and sew.

6 Place the pieces right sides together and sew, making sure that the zipper is open. Otherwise you won't be able to turn the bag around.

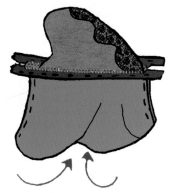

7 Turn the bag around. Use the end of a spoon to push out the corners.

voila

with Karen Weidner of *Karen Weidner Accessoires*

Karen Weidner Accessoires
Thalkirchner Straße 7
80337 München
www.karenweidner.de
info@karenweidner.de

Karen Weidner creates amazing handbags; each one is unique. Growing up, she liked to make her own dollhouse accessories with needle and thread. She would have loved to have taken crafts classes at school, but unfortunately crafts were totally "out" at that time. This might explain why the trained fashion designer is no big fan of the sewing machine. She prefers to make her bag sculptures with hundreds of hand stitches.

When did you decide to launch your own business?

While I was studying, it became clear to me that I wanted to be independent. Of course, I didn't know what that meant! I simply wanted to make my own things. If you are employed by a company your have to limit yourself a lot. Making pattern designs is very expensive, so usually companies buy a standard pattern, change it a bit, and sell it as a new design. This is also true for accessories.

What inspires your designs?

I have loved sweets for as long as I can remember! It didn't matter what the main course was, the important thing was dessert. I love pralinés, cakes, and cookies in particular. It is fascinating to make pastries from felt, and everybody recognizes them.

What is your favorite piece from your current collection?

It's a raspberry roll, my favorite cake. My mother makes a lot of them for me.

What are your favorite materials?

Felt is great to work with; it does not fray, and it's also quite sturdy.

You make your own products. Have you ever considered having them manufactured?

In 2005 I was negotiating to produce in China. But then I realized that bags lose appeal when they are made with machines. I think one notices how the bags are made. I will stay with handmade bags.

How many hours do you put into one model?

It takes about a week to make one model—longer if you include design time.

Your bags are almost like small works of art or couture. Are your models being sold in classic boutiques or even in galleries?

The bags are sold through the Artedona mail order company. They were part of the Chocolate Exhibit at the Munich Café Luitpold, and they are also shown at coffee shops and galleries. They are also distributed via my website because it is difficult to negotiate a price for handmade pieces with dealers. The bags are priced between 390 and 550 Euros ($390 and $600). But I have a few lower-priced pieces in my collection, such as hair bands and other accessories.

How do you find your customers, and how do they find you?

Customers find me through local media such as newspaper articles or a TV story about my work, but the Web is my most important platform. I would like to start a blog soon. This way the customers can comment and have a part in the production. Customers' ideas often lead to new models.

What are the pros and cons of working at home?

It is great to be managing your own time, but you have to be very careful to stay focused! It's always good to have a deadline. Working at home can be lonely, and that's why I also like to teach.

You are teaching at the Munich Academy of Fashion & Design. What is your advice for students who graduate and want to jump into self-employment?

I suggest that artists first spend time gaining experience and contacts in the industry. Enter design competitions and draft a business plan. If you can't afford a bookkeeper, you will need to know how to manage that yourself. And if you are partnering with someone, it's important to clearly establish your roles, how you will distribute the money, and how much time each person will commit to the business. There's a big difference between being friends with someone and running a business together. At the very least, make sure you know how you'll pay the rent each month.

Karen Weidner

Picture Your Own Bag

For the extroverted fashionistas among us who want to make a statement with bold motifs, this parade of all-over-print bags is just the right choice. Even snobbish lifestyle editors at Fashion Week will glance at them over their iPhones. The bags shown here can also be made from solid-color leather or washed canvas.

Transparent tote

Pin-up makeup bag

XXL print tote

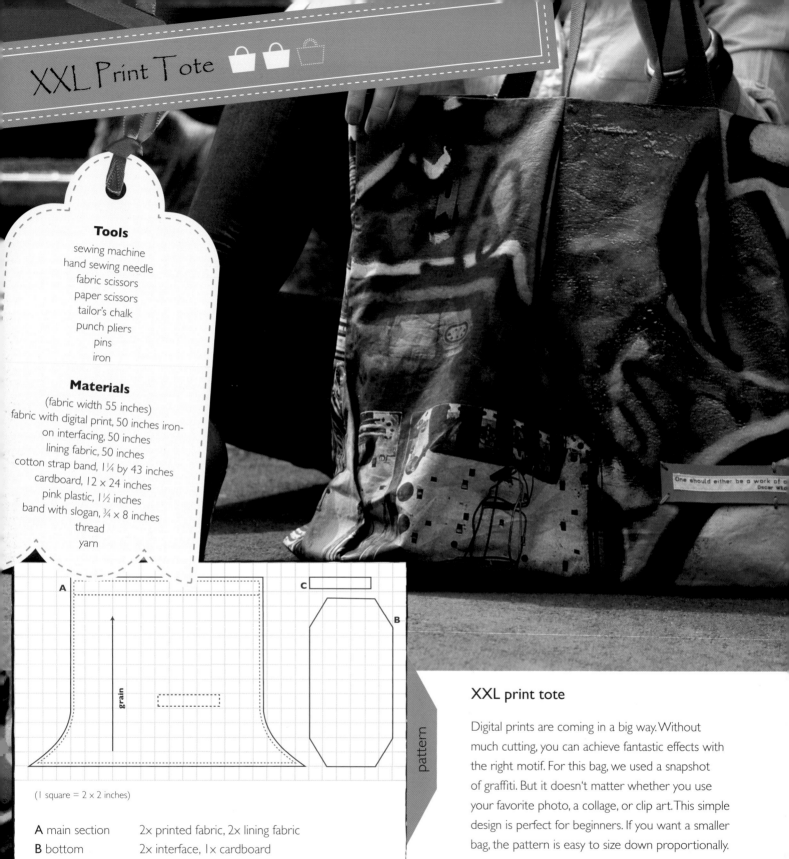

Tools

sewing machine
hand sewing needle
fabric scissors
paper scissors
tailor's chalk
punch pliers
pins
iron

Materials

(fabric width 55 inches)
fabric with digital print, 50 inches iron-on interfacing, 50 inches
lining fabric, 50 inches
cotton strap band, 1¼ by 43 inches
cardboard, 12 × 24 inches
pink plastic, 1½ inches
band with slogan, ¾ × 8 inches
thread
yarn

grain

pattern

(1 square = 2 × 2 inches)

A main section   2x printed fabric, 2x lining fabric
B bottom   2x interface, 1x cardboard
C plastic badge   1x plastic badge

XXL print tote

Digital prints are coming in a big way. Without much cutting, you can achieve fantastic effects with the right motif. For this bag, we used a snapshot of graffiti. But it doesn't matter whether you use your favorite photo, a collage, or clip art. This simple design is perfect for beginners. If you want a smaller bag, the pattern is easy to size down proportionally.

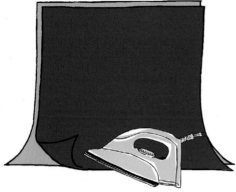

1 Enlarge and transfer the patterns and cut as indicated.

2 Iron the interfacing onto the A sections (printed fabric).

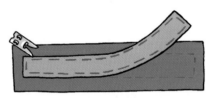

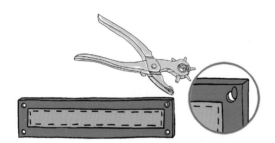

3 Sew the slogan band onto the plastic badge.

4 Use a punch pliers to make holes at the edges.

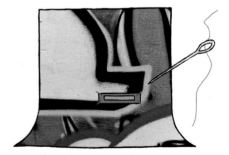

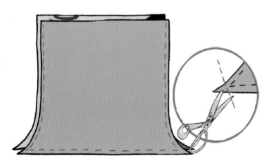

5 Sew the slogan band to the front of the bag, threading a needle of yarn through the punched holes (see marking on section A).

6 Sew the front and rear sections, right sides together, at the sides. Cut off the tips close to the seam.

7 Flip up the outer edges about 7½ inches and sew close to the seam.

8 Sew together the front and rear sections of the lining at the sides, leaving about 8 inches open at lower center. Cut off the lower tips close to the seam.

9 Fold and sew the edges of the lining as in step 7.

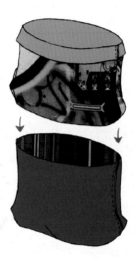

10 Fold the edge of the outer bag 2 inches toward the outside and place it into the inner lining with right sides together. Place the bag bottom B in between.

11 Sew together outer and inner bag at the upper edge.

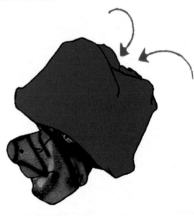

12 Pull the outer bag through the opening of the lining around to the right.

| 3 Close the lining opening.

| 4 For the handles, position the cotton strap band at each side of the bag, trim with the fabric, and sew.

| 5 Done.

Tip

Our design is perfect for a vivid digital print.

voilà

Tools

sewing machine
pins
fabric scissors
iron

Materials

(fabric width 55 inches)
brown imitation leather, 12 inches
motif fabric, 12 inches
optional edging, ½ by 16 inches
zipper, 13 inches
thread

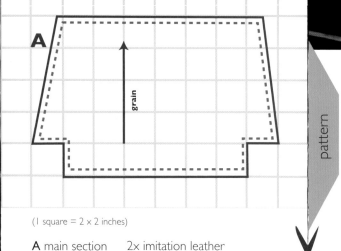

A

grain

(1 square = 2 × 2 inches)

A main section   2x imitation leather

pattern

Pin-up makeup bag

"Diamonds are a girl's best friend." Diamonds are pretty nice, but personally, I could not step outside without my best friends, mascara and lipstick. These helpers deserve a nice little bag. Our toiletries bag was inspired by the era of pin-up girls. We cut out the hot chicks from a pin-up fabric. Of course you can use other motifs such as flowers or animals and cut them from fabrics. Or, you can print your own fabric or work with flock print, or, or, or . . .

1 Enlarge and transfer section A and cut it out.

2 Cut the motifs from the printed fabric and place them on the front section.

3 Sew on the motifs with a zigzag stitch.

4 If you like, add edging and trim.

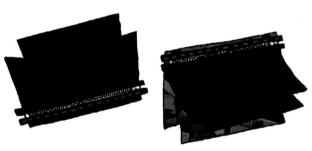

5 Sew the zipper between the front and rear sides.

6 Close the darts at the edges of the front and rear sections.

voila

7 Sew the front and rear sections, right sides together, and turn it around. You can find the instructions for the lipstick pendant on page 122.

8 Done!

Transparent Tote

Transparent Tote

Dream bags do not always have to be made from fabric. Designers since the 1960s have loved and used the futuristic look of plastics. Transparency is a phenomenon that appears repeatedly in bag collections from great designers, from Chanel to Louis Vuitton. However, our variation does not allow for a peek into the interior, which remains a secret for now. We prefer to put our favorite images between the walls of the bag and carry them everywhere we go.

Tools

glue stick
(not liquid glue)
sewing machine
pins
fabric scissors
pinking shears
paper scissors

Material

(fabric width 55 inches)
clear plastic, 34 inches
imitation leather, 12 inches
magazine clippings
and/or postcards
thread

pattern

(1 square = 2 × 2 inches)

A main section   4× clear plastic
B edging band   1× imitation leather
C handle   4× imitation leather

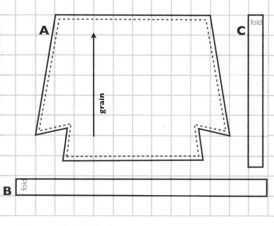

1 Cut the plastic to size and trim the edging band with pinking shears.

2 Cut out your favorite motifs from magazines (see also tip on page 86).

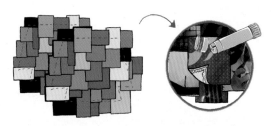

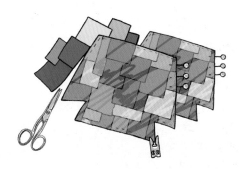

3 Arrange the motifs onto two pieces of paper so they are larger than section A, and use a glue stick to glue them together as one surface.

4 Place the plastic onto each paper section and sew the edges together. Cut away the extra paper.

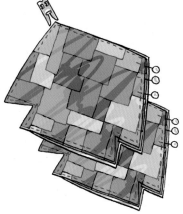

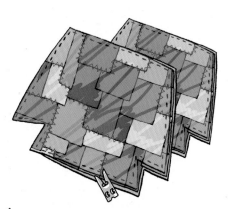

5 Place the other plastic pieces behind the paper sections so the paper lies between the two transparent sections. Sew all around again.

6 Sew together the front and rear section of the bag at the sides, right sides together. Cut away the lower tips close to the seam.

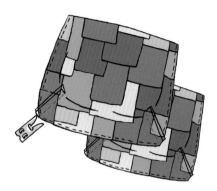

7 Sew the darts at the edges.

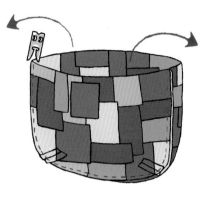

8 Sew the front and rear sections, right sides together, and carefully turn around.

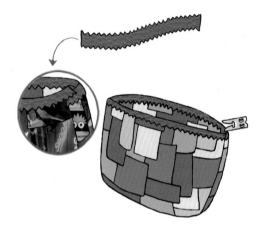

9 Place the edging around the bag's edge and topstitch on the right side.

10 For the handles, sew together two handle strips to form a ring.

Tip

Cutouts from newspapers, old photos, or a poster are fine for this bag as well. You can also place dried flowers between the plastic layers.

11 Turn to the right side and topstitch.

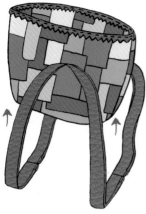

12 Position the handles on the bag, making sure the handle seams are on the bottom.

13 Stitch the handles to the bag along the upper edge of the bag.

14 Done! You will find the instructions for the monster pendant on page 121.

voilà

We recommend a glue stick for paper. Make sure it contains no solvents that might dissolve the plastic.

Tip

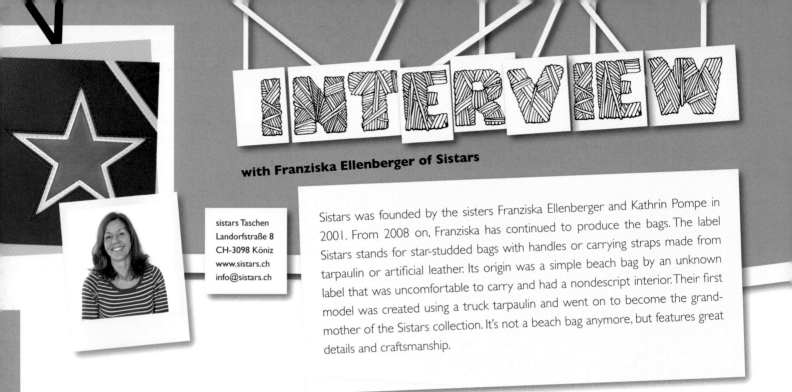

INTERVIEW

with Franziska Ellenberger of Sistars

sistars Taschen
Landorfstraße 8
CH-3098 Köniz
www.sistars.ch
info@sistars.ch

Sistars was founded by the sisters Franziska Ellenberger and Kathrin Pompe in 2001. From 2008 on, Franziska has continued to produce the bags. The label Sistars stands for star-studded bags with handles or carrying straps made from tarpaulin or artificial leather. Its origin was a simple beach bag by an unknown label that was uncomfortable to carry and had a nondescript interior. Their first model was created using a truck tarpaulin and went on to become the grandmother of the Sistars collection. It's not a beach bag anymore, but features great details and craftsmanship.

What is your professional background?

We are both trained furriers, and after a few years in the business we took different paths. My sister Kathrin worked in events and decoration. I studied pattern design and opened a studio in Konitz in 1989 for custom-made men's and women's fashion. So the infrastructure was already in place when we began designing our first bags.

You still manufacture each bag in your workshop. They are priced between 185 and 620 Swiss Francs ($200 and $663). Do you have a particular philosophy?

Because we make each bag from beginning to end, we always had the goal to offer our customers an individually distinctive bag, a philosophy that has worked well and distinguishes us from many bag-makers. I like the fact that we can always try out something new, work on old models, and discard this or that, and it helps not to need a large stock of bags. The disadvantage is that we have to have many different materials in stock and it is expensive to produce individual designs.

You offer customized shapes and colors. Do customers take advantage of this service?

Yes, quite a lot. Some of them have their own detailed ideas and others are inspired by the large selection. The catalog contains almost every bag ever made and is a great source of inspiration. I spend a lot of time talking with the customer. There is nothing more satisfying than matching the bag with the client, cutting it to size, sewing it, and handing it over personally.

You offer a wide spectrum of bags, from the simple carrying bag to the elaborate handbag with integrated side pockets and cellphone compartments. Do people gravitate to the elaborate models or do they lean more toward basic models?

Most clients already own several bags, so they almost always know what they want as to the interior compartments and features. Some like it really simple, others prefer to have many compartments for a wallet, water bottle, lipstick, and other items. Usually, the larger the bag, the more elaborate its interior.

Do you have a favorite model?

That would be Saggitarius (top right), a weekender with a few nice and functional details. The model for this bag was a piece from the 1960s inherited from my grandmother.

The Sistars label has been around since 2001. What have you learned about business partnerships?

After a few visits to trade fairs and large retailers, we learned about our limitations and what we consider important. We both realized that working with an outside manufacturer would be unacceptable, despite the amount of orders we were getting, and that we would not want to do so in the future, either. With this decision, it became more difficult to find resellers who were willing to invest the time it takes to discuss the bag with the client. It was also important to agree on financial matters, our salary, etc. We knew from the start that our concept would never make a lot of money. For this reason, we were very careful when it came to major invest-

ments such as opening our own store. We did not want to take on a lot of financial risk so that one of us could have the option of leaving Sistars at any time. This was actually helpful when my sister decided to dedicate herself to cooking, another passion. We have gone our separate ways in business, but we still spend time with each other.

sistars

Lovely Vintage Look

The use of vintage accessories is en vogue, letting these objects develop the charm of days gone by, either by emphasizing the patina effect or deliberately working with less precision. The following models feature this romantic-nostalgic touch: variations of round bags are adorned with small details from the sewing box.

Leo shopper

Betty bamboo

Rosalie's English roses

Marita's roll-up case

Zipper pochette

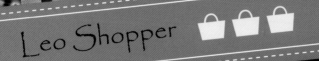
Tools

sewing machine
fabric scissors
tailor's chalk
pins
hand sewing needle
iron

Materials

(fabric width 55 inches)
imitation leopard skin, 12 inches
violet velvet, 10 inches
brown velvet, 6 inches
lining fabric, 18 inches
sewing tape, 55 inches
buttons
(perhaps leather and band scraps)
thread

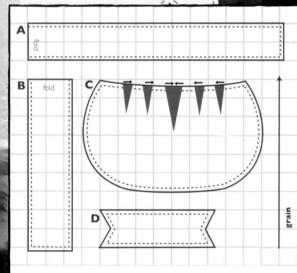

(1 square = 2 x 2 inches)

A handle	1x violet velvet	
B side section/bottom	1x brown velvet, 1x lining fabric	
C main section	2x imitation fur, 2x lining fabric	
D upper band	2x violet velvet	

Leo shopper

Leopard prints are tricky, as the pattern can be hard to pair with outfits. But we like to play around with clichés. Adorned with colorful buttons, the wildcat becomes domesticated.

1 Enlarge and transfer the patterns and cut as indicated.

2 Transfer the fold lines onto the C sections (fur and lining twice each) and fold where marked. If you prefer a firmer bag, iron inserts onto the C sections.

3 Stitch the upper edge to hold the folds in place.

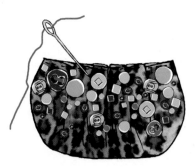

4 Sew the buttons to the front; reserve a few small ones for later.

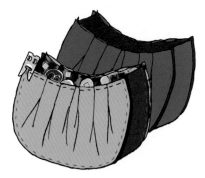

5 Sew the body of the bag together: sew the side section to the front and rear sections. Repeat with the lining.

6 Topstitch the side seam again.

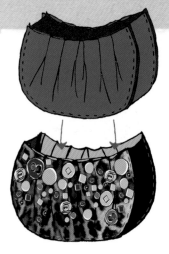

7 Place the lining into the outer bag.

8 With right sides together, sew the top velvet band D to the upper edge of the front and rear sections.

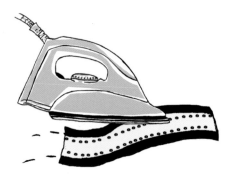

9 Flip inside and topstitch again.

10 Iron the handle onto sewing tape. The pattern will be wider than the tape insert.

11 Sew the handle into a ring and fold inward at the markings.

By the way ...

Expensive fur

In 1978 a Russian lynx fur coat, the most expensive ever published in the Neiman Marcus catalog, sold for $150,000 to an eccentric seventy-two-year-old woman in Rhode Island. Her will said that she wanted to be buried in it, too.

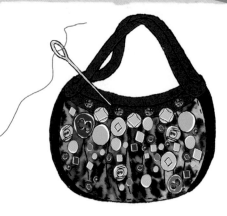

12   Pin the handle lengthwise and sew it.

13   Sew the remaining buttons to the top edge.

14   Done.

voilà

Tools

sewing machine
fabric scissors
hand sewing needle
pins
tailor's chalk

Materials

(fabric width 55 inches)
two-colored felt,
pink band,
1¼ x 98 inches
magenta band,
1 x 98 inches
2 bamboo handles
thread

A

B

C

grain

pattern

(1 square = 2 x 2 inches)

A main section   2x two-colored felt
B side section/bottom 2x two-colored felt
C flower   1x two-colored felt

Betty bamboo

Strong, durable bamboo is used as a handle. Its smooth texture contrasts nicely with the fuzzy felt. Alternatively, you can make your own ring handles, as shown on page 34.

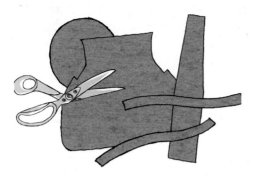

1 Enlarge and transfer the patterns and cut as indicated.

2 Sew on the bands. Their placement is your choice.

3 For more textural relief, cut additional strips from the felt scraps and apply them.

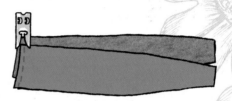

4 Sew together the bottom/side bands.

5 Now stitch on the right side.

6 Sew the bottom, front, and rear sections together.

7 Turn the bag around and topstitch the side seams.

8 Flip the seam allowances inside at the top and sew by hand.

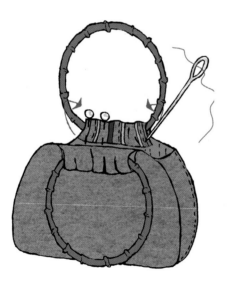

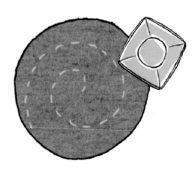

9 Fold the top around the bamboo handles and fold again from the inside. Sew by hand.

10 Mark flower with chalk as indicated.

Tip

Instead of purchasing ready-made bamboo handles, you can make your own (see page 34) .

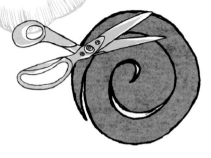

11 Cut along the spiral line.

12 Wrap the fabric around the handle to create a flower and tack down by hand.

13 Done.

voilà

Rosalie's English roses

Kitsch-lovers take note, retro flowers are hip again! The most popular are English roses that lend an English cottage look. Everyone recognizes these patterns on heavy fabric from grandma's sofa or curtains. Used to furnish an entire living room, they would feel overwhelming. However, used sparingly and combined with leather and felt leaves, these roses are a real eyecatcher.

Tools

sewing machine
fabric scissors
hand sewing needle
pins

Materials

(fabric width inches)
beige linen fabric, 16 inches
black lining fabric, 16 inches
beige imitation leather, 4 inches
motif fabric, 8 inches
beige cord, 71 inches
scraps from leather imitation and felt
thread

Templates

page 123

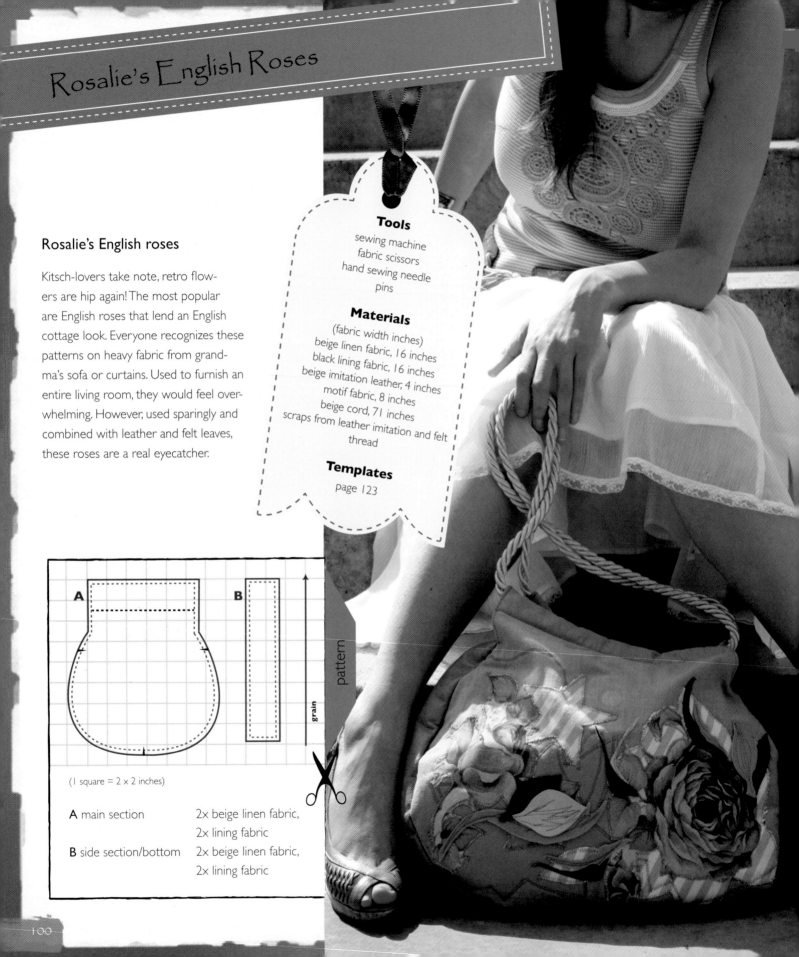

(1 square = 2 x 2 inches)

A — main section — 2x beige linen fabric, 2x lining fabric

B — side section/bottom — 2x beige linen fabric, 2x lining fabric

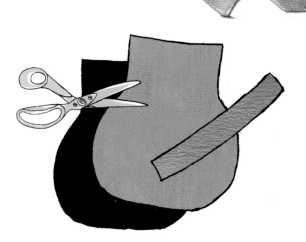

1 Enlarge and transfer the patterns and cut as indicated.

2 Cut roses for the appliqués from the motif fabric and lay them out on the front section. You can make more from scraps of leather and felt (see templates on page 123) and arrange them collage-like on the bag.

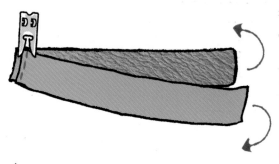

3 Outline the appliqués with matching thread and a zigzag stitch.

4 Sew together the bottom B sections at the center. Repeat with the lining fabric.

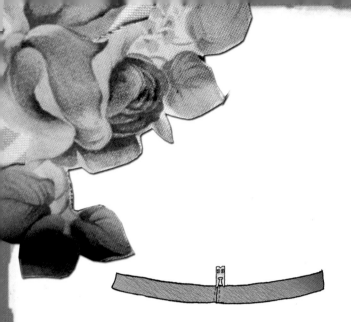

5 With the right side up, stitch on each side of the seam and repeat with the lining bottom.

6 Sew together the bottom, front, and rear sections, and repeat with the lining fabric.

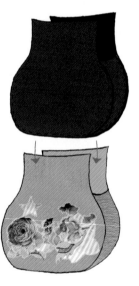

7 Now place the lining bag into the outer bag.

8 Fold the seam allowances of outer and lining bags at the upper edge and stitch with right sides together.

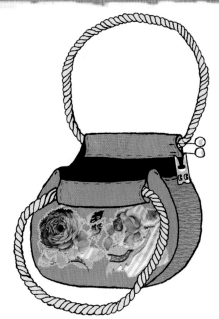

By the way . . .

Ur-handbag

The first handbag was developed at the beginning of the eighteenth century. Before that, ladies kept their coins and cosmetics in small pockets sewn into their wide skirts. There were also pouches sewn to the waistband. This way the valuable belongings were always close to the body. So it is no wonder that even modern women are always concerned about someone picking their handbag.

9   Sew the two ends of the cord together. Flip the upper edge of the bag inside over the cord and sew.

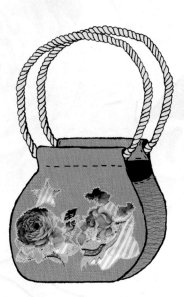

10   Done.

voilà

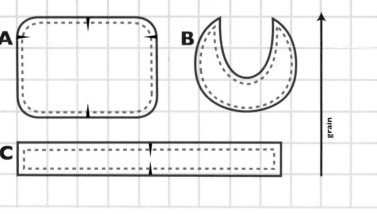

Tools

sewing machine
fabric scissors
hand sewing needle
pins

Materials

(fabric width 55 inches)
imitation leather, 14 inches
zipper, 32 inches
zipper, 10 inches
red band, ¾ × 8 inches
bracelet
thread

A

B

C

grain

pattern

(1 square = 2 × 2 inches)

A main section	2x imitation leather
B valance	4x imitation leather
C side section/bottom	1x imitation leather

Zipper pochette

The zipper pochette is a typical item of its time. Apparent contradictions unite for a new look: feminine, yet somehow it rocks. Its practical bracelet allows you to wear this elegant city companion around your wrist. With your hands free, you are certain to attract the attention of your neighbors at the coffee shop.

1 Enlarge and transfer patterns and markings and cut as indicated.

2 Cut the long zipper (32 inches) in half and pull the sections apart.

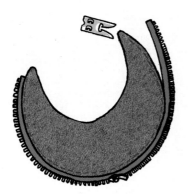

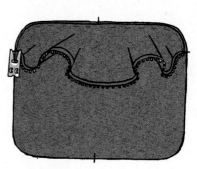

3 Place one of the valances onto a zipper section from step 2 and stitch from the outside. Repeat with the remaining three zipper sections and valances.

4 Sew the first valance onto the bag: the valance is placed at the left and right markings of the zipper and sewn.

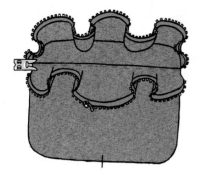

5 Sew the second valance onto the bag: flip up the first valance and pin the second valance at a distance of ¾-inch and sew.

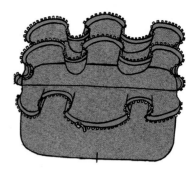

6 Sew the third valance onto the bag.

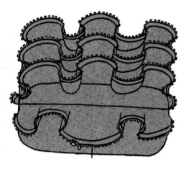

7 Sew the fourth valance onto the bag.

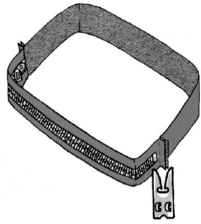

8 Sew the short zipper to the side section, right sides together.

Tip

If you don't happen to have a bracelet around, here is an alternative: leave the long loop (step 10) somewhat longer so you can fit it around your hand.

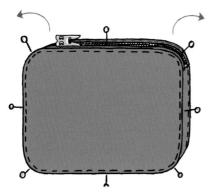

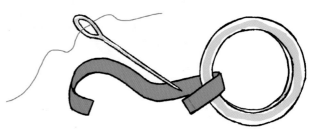

9 Sew together the side, front, and rear sections; observe the markings.

10 Place the red band around the bracelet and sew a small loop by hand.

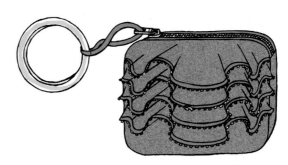

11 Pull the open end of the band through the zipper and sew it to the loop.

12 Done.

voilà

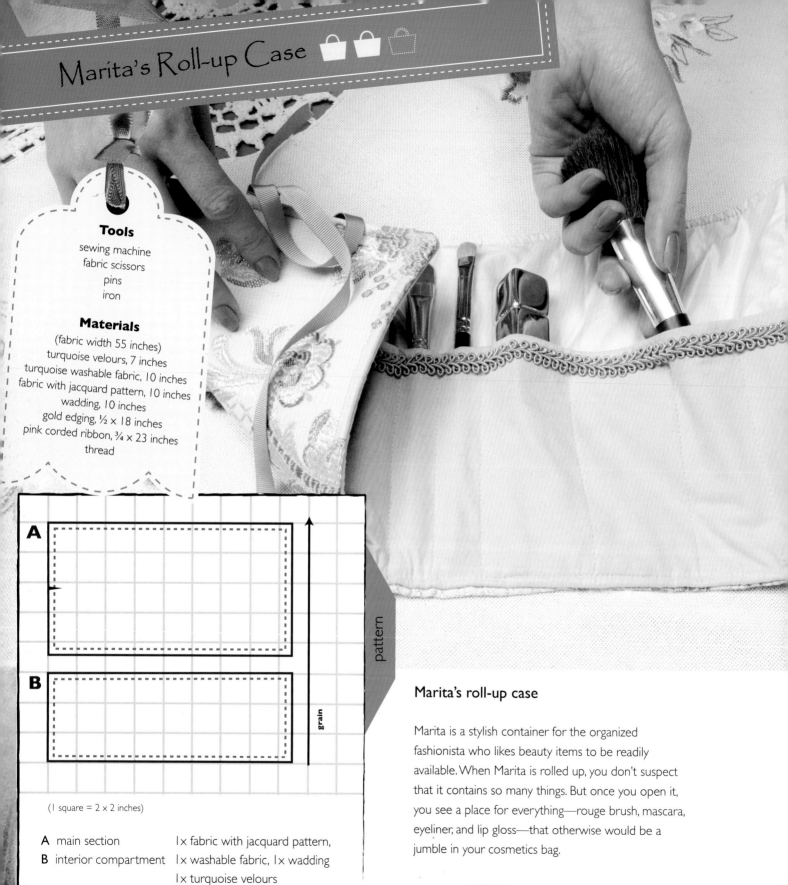

Tools

sewing machine
fabric scissors
pins
iron

Materials

(fabric width 55 inches)
turquoise velours, 7 inches
turquoise washable fabric, 10 inches
fabric with jacquard pattern, 10 inches
wadding, 10 inches
gold edging, ½ × 18 inches
pink corded ribbon, ¾ × 23 inches
thread

A

B

pattern

grain

(1 square = 2 × 2 inches)

A	main section	1× fabric with jacquard pattern,
B	interior compartment	1× washable fabric, 1× wadding
		1× turquoise velours

Marita's roll-up case

Marita is a stylish container for the organized fashionista who likes beauty items to be readily available. When Marita is rolled up, you don't suspect that it contains so many things. But once you open it, you see a place for everything—rouge brush, mascara, eyeliner, and lip gloss—that otherwise would be a jumble in your cosmetics bag.

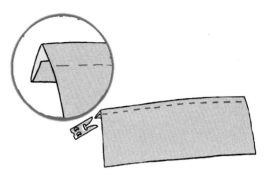

1 Enlarge and transfer the patterns and cut as indicated.

2 Section B will serve later as the interior compartment. Fold it under twice ½-inch at the upper edge and sew.

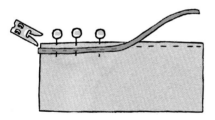

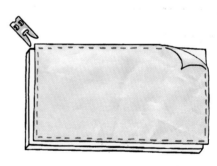

3 Pin the gold edging to the top edge of the right side of section B and sew.

4 Narrowly stitch the washable fabric A to the wadding.

By the way ...

For those who carry a sketchbook, Marita's roll-up case is also great for storing pencils and pens.

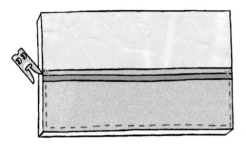

5 Place the inner compartment B on the lower edge of main section A and sew.

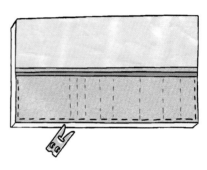

6 Now stitch individual compartments to section B, leaving a minimum width of ¾-inch. The stitches should not reach higher than the edging, or the openings will be too tight.

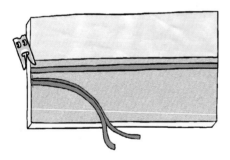

7 Sew the corded band close to the right edge.

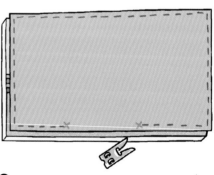

8 With right sides together, sew the finished inner section of the case to the jacquard-patterned fabric, leaving a 3-inch opening at the lower center. The corded band lies between the pattern sections. Turn the case right-side-out.

By the way . . .

Instructions for the matching Kelly bag are available as a free download (see page 155).

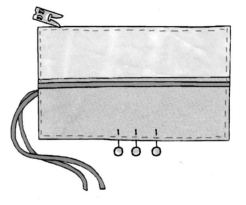

9 Fasten the opening with pins and stitch all around the case, closing the opening.

10 Iron the case on low heat. Done.

voila

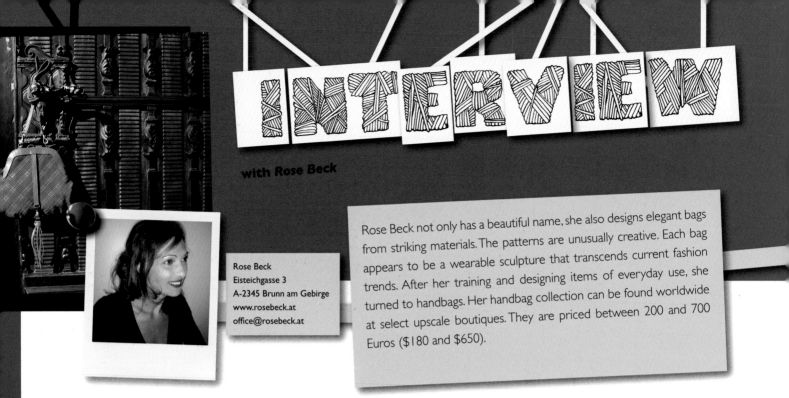

INTERVIEW

with Rose Beck

Rose Beck
Eisteichgasse 3
A-2345 Brunn am Gebirge
www.rosebeck.at
office@rosebeck.at

Rose Beck not only has a beautiful name, she also designs elegant bags from striking materials. The patterns are unusually creative. Each bag appears to be a wearable sculpture that transcends current fashion trends. After her training and designing items of everyday use, she turned to handbags. Her handbag collection can be found worldwide at select upscale boutiques. They are priced between 200 and 700 Euros ($180 and $650).

Where do you find inspiration for your unique bags and materials?

I collect ideas when visiting trade shows and try to develop my own items. The bags should differentiate themselves from mass-produced pieces and yet be wearable and sophisticated.

What is the typical design process for a Rose Beck handbag?

I design on paper, determine the size, and make a rough prototype from imitation leather to check the proportions. Then I pass it on to prodution and they create the templates. We check those together, make changes, and make the first sample. If everything went right, it turns out perfect.

Where can we see your gems?

At Austrian leather shops and boutiques, and in Belgium, Japan, Hong Kong, Dubai, and others.

What is your favorite bag from your collection?

It's the *Berlin* model (top right).

Your bags have a high-quality finish. Are you manufacturing yourself or having them made by another company?

The bags are always made in a professional manufacturing facility.

Tell us about your experience with foreign manufacturers. What are the advantages and disadvantages?

The advantages are that their professional workshops are larger compared to Austria, materials such as leather and accessories are easier to order on short notice, and they have good, experienced craftsmen. Disadvantages are the distance, foreign language and mentality, and transportation costs.

What has been your experience with the large international fairs and conventions that you visit regularly? Is it worth investing a small fortune to exhibit your work, or is it better for new businesses to focus on smaller exhibitions?

I recommend starting out small and focusing on national exposure. Once you become established, it makes more sense to visit international fairs. However, make sure you will be able to fulfill the volume of orders you expect. Also consider whether you will be able to finance at least a few subsequent visits to a particular fair, even if orders are low the first year. Try to avoid borrowing money to attend shows.

Tell us an interesting anecdote about exhibiting at a fair.

At one presentation of a new collection, I was wearing a prototype bag that was not part of the collection. I had put it under a table when a Japanese retailer dropped by, looked at the collection, and found my hidden bag. He grabbed it and was so excited that this model made up most of his order. His instincts were right. It went on to become a bestseller.

Rose Beck

Graffiti bag

Slipcover bag

Monster pendant

Pimp My Bag

From hopelessly outdated to fashion forward:
Is there an item from Aunt Gertrude's estate or an unusual purse in
your attic that is out of style, but which you are not ready to throw
away? With just a few steps, a painless facelift will catapult it into a
new age. No sewing required—just a hot glue gun and paint brush.

Lipstick pendant

Fruit basket

Sleeping Beauty's wake-up kit

Fabric brooch

Tools

hot glue gun

Materials

bag with clip fastener
small fabric flowers
vintage button

voilà

Sleeping Beauty's wake-up kit

Small evening bags with a clip fastener are going through a major revival and feature ultra-feminine touches. The small, cuddly accessory reminds us of the glorious bygone days of glamorous movie divas and their bright red lips. Bags and lipstick cases make the same seductive click when they are opened and closed. They suffered the same fate—the evening bag was replaced with the clutch, the lipstick with lip gloss. To celebrate the feminine, we are decorating with an armful of flowers. This bag is an eyecatcher on the delicate arm of its wearer.

before

fabric flowers

1 Fill the bag fully to plump it out.

2 Glue on the fabric flowers one by one with the hot glue gun.

3 Glue the vintage button onto the clip.

4 Let it dry. Done.

Tools

sewing machine
fabric scissors
glue stick

Material

old bag
1–2 packs of photos
fabric
(see tip)
long strap
thread

Slipcover bag

You can give new life to an old bag whose shape you like simply by encasing it in a new cover. The new pattern pieces should be a little larger than the original bag to accommodate seam allowances.

1 Measure the bag's body and transfer the measurements onto pattern paper. Or simply place the bag onto the paper and trace its outline with a pencil.

2 Transfer the pattern onto fabric and add a ½-inch seam allowance all around. The upper edge should get a little more seam allowance (about 1½-inches) .

3 Cut out the sections and sew them together. Add loops for the left and right handles. The loops should face the inner side so they are outside when the bag is turned around.

4 Fold the seam allowance at the upper edge in to the left side and sew. Pull the new bag cover over the original bag and hand-stitch close to the side seams.

5 If you like, remove the old strap from a handbag and fasten it to the new bag. Done.

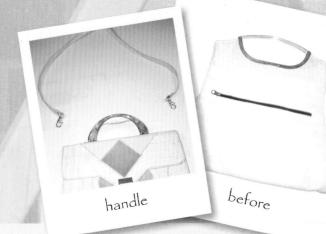

handle

before

voilà

Tools

brush

Materials

old army bag
white acrylic paint
masking tape
brown marker
clear lacquer

original

masked

painted

Graffiti bag

Most designer handbags can't compare with the quality of a handmade Swiss army bag. Once they were used to store bullets and ammunition, and today you can get good deals on them at second-hand shops. Often, a stamp on the fastener indicates the origin and year of manufacture. We couldn't resist experimenting with this classic bag. We also wanted to open the world of bags to men using paint and imagination.

1 Remove residual dust from the bag and carefully cover the leather with masking tape.

2 Paint with white acrylic paint; you may need to apply more than one coat.

3 Remove the tape and apply large patterns with a brown marker. Then seal the bag with a clear, chemical-free lacquer. Done.

Sporty

Did you know that a private first-class soldier is called an Adidas soldier because of the three slanted stripes on his badge?

Fruit basket

Perhaps you have not yet achieved your optimal bikini silhouette, despite dieting. But why cover yourself up when you can create a sweet distraction with this low-calorie-fruit beach basket. It will be the envy of all those skinny models.

before

1 Remove the handles from the straw bag.

2 Wrap the handles with the checkered fabric (see page 34).

3 Use the templates on page 123 to cut melon and strawberry shapes from leather or imitation leather. Glue on the beading with textile glue.

4 Place the fruit pieces onto the basket and glue with a hot glue gun.

5 Glue the red band to the edge of the bag so that ½-inch of fabric sticks out.

6 Sew small loops from the checkered band fabric and use them to attach the handles on the outside of the basket.

Tools
scissors
hot glue gun
textile glue
hand sewing needles
scissors

Materials
old straw bag
imitation leather
beads
checkered band
red band
thread

Picnic basket
Picnics are popular in England. Queen Victoria liked to eat outdoors. Around the nineteenth century the picnic basket became popular. England's upper classes still love a picnic, especially at social events like horse racing in Ascot, or the Wimbledon tennis tournament.

voila

Fabric Brooch

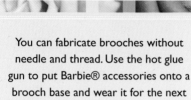

voilà

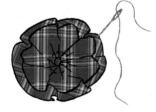

You can fabricate brooches without needle and thread. Use the hot glue gun to put Barbie® accessories onto a brooch base and wear it for the next festive event with a touch of humor.

Tools

sewing machine
sewing needle
hot glue gun

Materials

(fabric width 55 inches)
patterned fabric, 7 inches
brooch base
green felt, 3 x 5 inches
2 buttons, ½ to ¾-inch
satin band, ½ x 16 inches
satin band, ½ x 16 inches
thread

Templates, page 123

Fabric brooch

Jazz up your handbag with an opulent brooch. This brooch works best for fabric bags, as it is difficult to perforate a leather bag without damaging it. Grab a brooch base and glue gun and let your fantasies run wild.

1 Fold the fabric strip lengthwise and stitch the open edge by hand or with a sewing machine. Leave the thread hanging at both ends.

2 Gather the band by pulling it along the threads.

3 Twist the ruffled band into a rosette and fasten with a few stitches.

Brooch bases are available at arts and crafts retailers or online shops such as Etsy.

4 Add small ornaments like bows, buttons, and brooches.
If you like, use the oak leaf template on page 123.

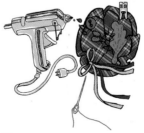

5 Attach your chosen decorations with a hot glue gun or sew them by hand.

6 Glue the rosette onto the brooch base with a hot glue gun. Done.

Monster pendant

Our monster is crazy about bags and slightly dazed by shopping frenzies, so it is a bit cross-eyed, but obviously quite happy!

Tools
sewing machine
fabric scissors
hand sewing needle

Materials
green leather imitation, 8 × 4 inches
black cotton, 8 × 4 inches
white cotton, 4 × 4 inches
cotton batting, 8 × 4 inches
pink patent leather, 1¼ × 1¼ inches
1 eyelet, ½-inch
chain, 6½ inches
thread

Templates
page 123

1 Transfer the patterns from page 123. Cut the base circle from imitation leather, two small circles from white cotton, the heart from patent leather, and the remaining sections from black cotton.

2 Sew the head and ear onto the green base circle. For the eyes, place the black pupils onto the white background and sew by hand. Embroider the mouth with thread or yarn and sew on the speech bubble.

3 Sew the heart and letters onto the speech bubble, close to the edge.

4 Sew together the front and back, leaving a small opening. Push the cotton batting into the opening and close by hand.

5 Punch in the eyelet as indicated on the package instructions, pull the chain through, and done!

voilà

121

voilà

Tools

sewing machine
fabric scissors
glue stick

Materials

black imitation leather, 4 x 4 inches
pink imitation leather, 2 x 2 inches
silver imitation leather, 2 x 2 inches
band, ½ x 8 inches
1 eyelet, ½-inch
thread

Templates

page 123

Lipstick pendant

The lipstick pendant not only looks great with our cosmetics bag, it signals: proud to be a woman!

1 Transfer the patterns and cut them out: two black lipstick holders, two pink lipsticks, and two small silver bars.

2 Place the pink and silver leather pieces onto the two black lipstick forms and carefully sew.

3 Glue front and rear sections together.

4 Cut a small hole for the eyelet into the round section of the pendant and punch it as shown on the package instructions.

5 Now thread a band through the eyelet and you've got your lipstick pendant.

Here you will find templates for the bag motifs in their actual size. Simply trace and transfer the pattern onto your fabric.

Deer Motif

Weekender

Rosalie's English Roses

Fruit Basket

Fabric Brooch

Monster Pendant

Lipstick Pendant

INTERVIEW

with Sabine Spanheimer of Stulle

stulle
stulle shop
raumerstr. 34
10437 Berlin
www.stulle-berlin.de
mail@stulle-berlin.de

The children of Berlin inspire Sabine Spanheimer's bag creations: unconventional, practical, and with a great sense of humor. Because the abstract appliqués are individually sewn with wild sewing machine stitches, no two bags are exactly alike. Sabine created the label Stulle six years ago. The colorful bags and wallets are sold from Japan to Vancouver; the bags cost between 45 and 98 Euros ($40 and $90).

When did you decide to start your own business?
In mid-2004, after working for years in design studios in Berlin, I decided to produce my own ideas. I simply could not imagine continuing to work for someone else.

Who are your customers?
People who love modern design, and parents and grandparents with a sense of humor.

Did your formal design training prepare you for running a business?
When I studied graphic design, there was no education in what it means to be independent.

Your unique pieces are made entirely by hand in Berlin. Why did you decide against a likely cheaper mass production service abroad?
I can keep an eye on production and react quickly if there are problems. Also, our products cannot be produced in mass quantities because our seamstresses contribute their own creativity by choosing fabrics and colors within a given design. This is the only way that every piece can be unique.

You also use scraps of packaging and found objects for your bags and wallets. How do you acquire these materials, and what is your philosophy of choosing materials?
I use objects and materials that stand out for their surface texture, color, or pattern. I love garage sales, whether they are in Berlin or a Bavarian village I am passing through. I don't rummage around Berlin's trash cans; however, when I started out I salvaged scraps from the large trash containers of an awning manufacturer.

You are selling your products worldwide. What is the Internet's role in distribution and sales?
The distribution is organized through our production processing. Retailers contact me online with questions about pricing and ordering. They place orders on the website's retailer page.

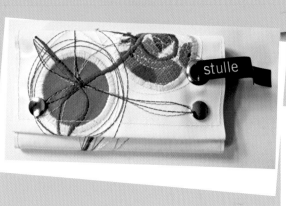

Could you share a story about your experiences working with customers or suppliers?

Not long ago, a retailer ordered ten wallets on the website, all of them in white. I thought: "Well, pretty smart, the white ones always sell well; he will have no trouble finding buyers." When his order arrived, he called me on the phone, screaming that he had received only white wallets. I calmly explained that we had not made a mistake. He argued, so I sent him a screen shot of his order. A day later, the retailer sent me an email complaining about the bimbo on the phone, whom he would have fired a long time ago. I thought "Well, if that were to happen, there wouldn't even be white wallets to buy."

Then there have been some lovely, funny suggestions for motifs for the kindergardener bag, such as an electric guitar, a tangerine, and a sheep with a spinning wheel.

Recycle Mania

If you liked the ideas in *Pimp My Bag,* you'll appreciate this chapter. The following models bring new meaning to the notion of recycling. Items marked by time can now be reincarnated into bag nirvana. Whether it's an umbrella smashed by a gale, a favorite old pair of jeans, or the **Dirty Dancing** video that you played a thousand times, all of your ex-favorites are here.

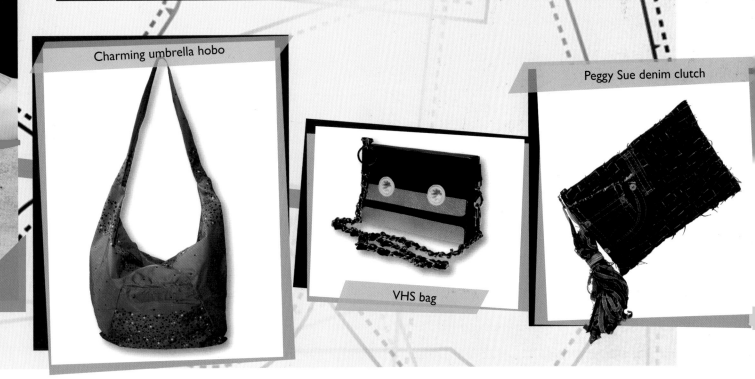

Charming umbrella hobo

VHS bag

Peggy Sue denim clutch

Charming umbrella hobo

There's so much you can do with an old umbrella! We love all of our bag children, but this nifty model is our biggest source of pride. It is multi-use, light as a feather, and tucks easily into a pocket or purse when not in use, so you are always prepared for a spontaneous trip to the supermarket. The pattern is designed so that the entire umbrella is used except for the metal skeleton, which you could use to dry lingerie in an emergency.

Tools

sewing machine
pins
iron
seam ripper
fabric scissors

Materials

old pocket umbrella
Velcro band, ¾ × 4 inches
thread

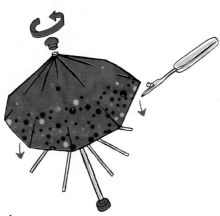

1 Remove the umbrella fabric from the metal frame.

2 Separate the individual triangles with the seam ripper or small scissors and iron on low temperature.

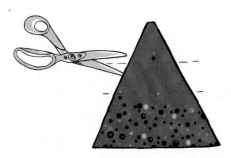

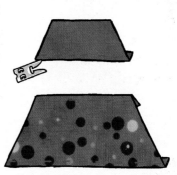

3 Divide one of the eight triangles in half lengthwise, and halve it again. We don't need the tip anymore.

4 The larger section will become a pouch. The smaller section will become the flap. Fold the seam allowances ½-inch as shown and sew.

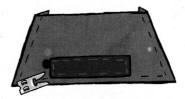

5 Fold the side seams of the flap and sew.

6 Sew one of the Velcro bands onto the right side of the flap.

Different places, different customs
While we tend to run to the beach to get a tan at the slightest sign of sunshine, women in countries such as Japan still use portable umbrellas to protect themselves from the hot sun.

By the way ...

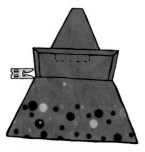

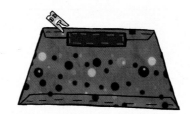

7 Sew the shorter edge of the finished flap with Velcro to another triangle with right sides together, placing it above the center.

8 Sew the other half of the Velcro to the "wrong" side of the pouch of step 4.

9 Topstitch the pouch onto the triangle. Place the pouch so that the shorter edge is abutting the shorter edge of the flap.

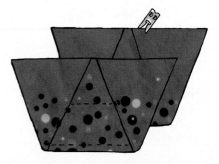

10 Trim the extra fabric on both sides.

11 Sew the open sides of the pouch closed (close to the edge) so the pouch folds over the flap opening.

12 Sew together two sets of three triangles to create the front and rear section. The triangle with the pouch is at front center.

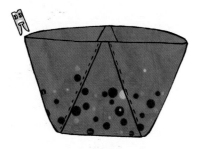

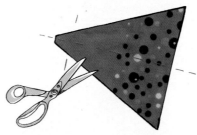

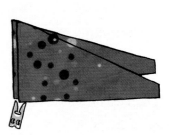

13 Sew together the front and rear sections, right sides together, then turn right side out.

14 Cut the remaining triangle along the dotted lines. The upper tip is not needed anymore.

15 These two handle sections are sewn together at their wide sides. Fold apart and iron.

16 Fold the handle lengthwise, fold the ends and the seam allowance, and sew.

17 Sew the handles to the outside of the bag so the seam points inward.

18 Tuck flap into pouch. Done.

19 Store the bag in the outer pouch.

20 The compact emergency companion is now finished.

voilà

folded

VHS Bag

Tools

hand sewing needle
pins
fabric scissors
tailor's chalk
felt pen
hot glue gun
cutter
punch pliers
screwdriver

Materials

(fabric width 55 inches)
black imitation leather, 6 inches
silver tape or fabric, 1½ inches
metal chain, 43 inches
black band, 1/2 × 63 inches
2 snap hooks
2 D-rings
2 brass fasteners (office supplies)
video cassette with box
thread

VHS bag

The era of the VHS tape has come to an end, and if your parents have given you an embarrassing tape from their high school dance, we have a great idea to spare you the shocking trip into the past. By the way, we are not the first to come up with this concept: it was inspired by the 2009 cassette bag by Chanel.

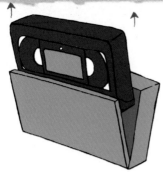

1 Remove the cassette from its box.

2 Unscrew the cassette and remove its interior. You will need the white spools later.

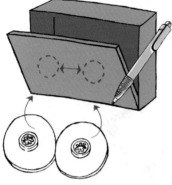

3 On the box, draw two circles as large as the inner white cassette spools, placing them about 2½ inches apart, and cut them out.

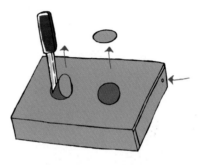

4 On each side, mark one hole ¾-inch below the top edge, and punch or cut out. The holes will be used later to attach the handles.

5 Push the interior white cassette spools into the holes and fasten with a few drops of hot glue.

6 Trace all parts of the box onto the leather. Then make two 3 x 1-inch loops where the handles will be attached and mark the appliqué outlines on the silver tape or fabric.

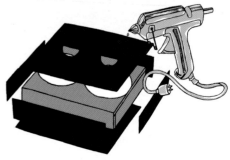

7   Cut out the marked parts.

8   Glue on the black sections to the box with hot glue. Be careful not to glue the cassette so it can easily be opened and closed.

9   Now glue on the silver sections and open the side hole you glued shut.

10   Thread the black band through the chain.

11   Wrap the band around the ring at the snap hook and sew by hand with a few stitches.

12   Wrap the loops around the snap hook ring and glue them to the ring.

13 Punch or cut one hole into each loop.

14 It is best to attach the handles twice: with a drop of glue and with a brass fastener.

15 Done.

voilà

Peggy Sue Denim Clutch

Tools

sewing machine
fabric scissors
paper scissors
hand sewing needle
tape

Material

old jeans
zipper, about 10 inches
edging, ¾ x 12 inches
cardboard
thread

Peggy Sue denim clutch

If you Google "bags made from jeans," you'll see a sight of sheer horror: lower torsos amputated at the legs, with handles! There must be a better way to turn your favorite jeans into a bag. After a lot of experimentation, we succeeded in making a casual but distinctive clutch. With its weaving technique, this model is an eye-catcher. The slightly frazzled "raw edge" will appeal to even those who prefer understatement.

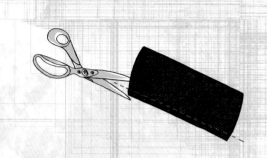

1 Cut off both pant legs.

2 Cut the legs along the double seam.

3 Cut one of the legs into strips ¾-inch wide.

4 Snip the cardboard every inch on each side.

5 Stretch the denim strips and fasten the ends on the back with tape.

6 Weave the strips.

For a luxurious Bottega-Veneta look, cut your old leather coat into strips and use our simple technique to weave them into a new fabric.

Tip

7 Tack down the woven material with a few hand stitches around the perimeter.

8 Remove the woven surface from the cardboard and trim the strips so the edges are even.

9 Remove one of the top pockets from the remaining pants.

10 Fold under the rounded edge and stitch to the top left of the front section.

11 Place the zipper at the top edge, right sides together, and sew.

12 Now fold the woven fabric, right sides together, into a clutch and sew the second side of the zipper.

13 Sew the sides together.

14 Trim the corners, open the zipper, and flip it right-side-out.

15 Cut the second pant leg into ¼-inch strips for the side tassel.

16 Reserve one strip, make a bundle with the rest, and wrap the strip around them at the center.

17 Fasten with a matching or contrasting material.

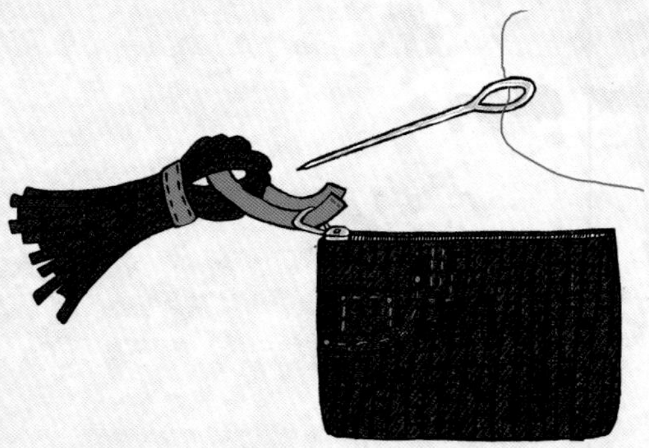

18 Pull a 5-inch loop through the tassel and zipper opening and sew together.

19 Done.

voilà

By the way ...

Texas pants

Jeans used to be called Texas pants in Germany. From 1953 on, the first jeans for women were manufactured for European markets. These girl's camping pants had a side zipper.

INTERVIEW

with Karin Maislinger of Kontiki

kontiki
Karin Maislinger
Grundsteingasse 38/4
A - 1160 Wien
www.kontiki.or.at
buero@kontiki.or.at

Karin Maislinger was born in Salzburg and grew up in Bad Wimsbach-Neydharting. After attending a fashion college in Linz, Austria, she moved to Vienna to study landscaping. In 2003, she founded Kontiki and started to design bags from recycled bike tubes. Karin Maislinger lives and works in Vienna. Her own small workshop is located in the Ottakring area of Vienna.

Where can we see your bags, and how much do they cost?

You can see them in our Vienna workshop and other Vienna shops such as Ozelot and das möbel, as well as at national and international fairs. We are working on setting up a small distribution network in Europe. The wallets cost around 50 Euros ($55); large bags cost 120–200 Euros ($130–$220). Travel bags are 220–260 Euros ($243–$287).

What is your favorite piece from the current collection?

That would be the *Komet* model (top right), a bag I designed for my first plane trip last year. I like the accessibility in the lower section and the bag's versatility. The top section holds a notebook and small items. The middle section can be removed.

Why did you name your company Kontiki?

The name is based on the raft made by Thor Heyerdahl, who sailed from the West Coast of the US to Polynesia in the 1940s. I had bought a book about it at a garage sale and was impressed by the courage of this wild, bearded crew. I thought Kontiki would be a good name for my own adventure. I created the label in 2003, and the brand is registered internationally.

You are using bike tubes and tires to make your bags. How did you arrive at using these interesting raw materials, and what are their advantages?

I have been using old bike tubes since 2003. The idea came when I was working for a bike messenger company in Vienna. The unused tubes are often as good as new and make a good base material for waterproof, sturdy containers.

Many of your bags are made in your own workshop. How do you create a bag?

The Kontiki bags are made in our own small workshop. We also make the first prototypes here, as well as small editions of individual models. Our workshop is kind of minimalist. We work with a few industrial sewing machines, and that's pretty much it. We also customize our bags for clients. Our focus is on a perfect finish. For this reason, many of the seams are doubled with special reinforcements. This increases the cost of production, but it makes a lot of sense to us.

You decided to produce small editions and one-off models, rather than do mass production. How did you arrive at this decision, and is it worth the expense to manufacture on your own?

When you have a fashion background and start your own label, it is customary to make the first model yourself. When I began, I simply had no money to hire someone else to make them. Once production takes off, you realize that it is not easy to keep the quality high. Even when you use national workshops, you really have no influence as the contractee. So I realized that the only way to control the quality during the entire manufacturing process was to define the standards and create my own workshop.

Your business focuses on ecologically minded products made from recycled materials. Do customers value these characteristics?

I think the interest in ecological products has increased, but it is hard to say whether there is a general change in consumer habits. My impression is that you tend to buy "green" when you are more conscious about the issues. However, our products are not just about the recycled content. I think our customers value the design, small editions, local production, and the craftsmanship and unusual materials.

kontiki

Ask Aunt Nani

What you always wanted to know about bags, but were afraid to ask.

Dear aunt Nani,

I love my XXL tote and feel horrible whenever I have to leave home without all of my stuff. Evening bags are always too small, and it is hard to choose what to leave behind. What items do you consider essentials?

Regards, Jasmin

Dear Jasmin,

There is a quick answer to your question: you really only need your credit card, cellphone, keys, powder, and gloss. At first it might be difficult to rid yourself of all the riff-raff. But you will enjoy the freedom and the dance floor without the usual baggage.

Enjoy!

Regards, Aunt Nani

Dear Aunt Nani,

One can never have too many bags. However, the choices are overwhelming. What are the basic essentials? Are there must-haves in the world of bags?

Regards, Alexandra

Dear Alexandra,

A bag should be primarily an expression of your personality, whether it is a bright green shopping bag or a colorfully patterned babushka tote. As a basic bag, we suggest a black, medium-sized bag that you can tuck under your arm. It might also be caramel-colored, olive, mustard, or taupe. During summer you will need a lighter alternative to leather, so canvas bags, either solid color or a floral print, are the ideal complement. Finally, you will need an evening bag: a black clutch is best, and perhaps another one with straps in a neutral color. These small clutches look great in purple, pink, gold, and white.

Regards, Aunt Nani

Dear Aunt Nani,

I am about to order the latest fabrics and materials and finally sit down at the sewing machine. Although I am sparing with colorful designs, I am bolder with accessories. Is there a color I should avoid?

Your Jessika

Dear Jessika,

If the accessories match the outfit, all colors are permitted. With bags, this is more of the seasonal issue. If you choose olive instead of kiwi-green, your bag may be hip year-round. Be careful with white and pastel colors: once winter comes, the item will only work if it is worn with a white hat and light-colored coat. Whatever materials you choose, we wish you a lot of fun while sewing.

Regards, Aunt Nani

Dear Aunt Nani,

I am asking for help because my mother and I cannot agree: should you match the bag to the outfit, or the other way around?

Regards, Vivi

Dear Vivi,

You should match the bag to the outfit, because the clothing style does not have to match the bag; rather, the two should complement each other. For example, Betty bamboo might look plain with a suit, but with old jeans and a tank top it suddenly looks cool. The Peggy Sue denim clutch looks best with a classic outfit. Fashion is like love: contrasts are more interesting than complete harmony. This may also be true for a mother-daughter relationship.

Regards, Aunt Nani

P.S. Always make the bag first, then buy the pumps. This will save you money, as shoes without a matching partner often gather dust in the closet.

Regards, Aunt Nani

Dear Aunt Nani,

I was given a decorative key chain for my birthday, but is too opulent for the keys. I was thinking about using it as a pendant for my drab leather bag. Is it hip to have something dangling from your bag?

Bianca

Dear Bianca,

Anything reminiscent of charm bracelets is out, and that means anything that jingles or dangles, including small chains, feathers, and pearls. These are totally dated. But brooches and buttons are fashionable; they are best used on a tote or messenger bag.

Tip: Hang the keychain on your car's rearview mirror and use brooches for all other bag decorations, maybe even homemade ones (see page 120).

Enjoy your creativity.

Regards, Aunt Nani

Dear Aunt Nani,

I often attend after-work parties close to the office. There's nothing better than to finish the day with a cocktail. Can I carry my large everyday bag, or will it look out of place?

Regards, Conny

Dear Conny,

Well, we don't want to be too strict about an after-work party. However, better not! What would happen if you were to be invited to a movie premiere or restaurant opening later? Better to use the paparazzi pochette (page 30), and in no time you will turn into the queen of the night. Here is another tip: the longer the skirt, the smaller the bag should be. Cocktail dresses look great with larger clutch bags. The bags look most elegant worn around the wrist.

Regards, Aunt Nani

Setting up a Business: When Your Hobby Turns into a Profession

Requirements

Be honest: how many creative people do you know who are seriously interested in the financial aspects of running a business? Do you know about overhead? Ever heard of liquidity planning (nothing to do with the drinks in the bar)?

A successful bag designer must be able to do more than develop designs. Before you dive in, study the legal and economic implications in detail.

Business plan

- Idea

- Summary

- Market analysis and overview

- Who are the founders? (qualifications?)

- Purchasing and manufacturing

- Sales and marketing

- Legal entity of business (sole proprietor, LLC, etc.)

- Financing plan (income and expenses)

- Benefits and risks

Tip: There are a multitude of contests for start-up businesses. Consider entering your business plan in a competition—perhaps you will even win a prize. Either way, competitions are a great resource for start-ups. Ask your bank and local business council for contest recommendations!

Compare operations with your business plan on a regular basis. Be critical! What works well and what does not? Update your business plan at least once a year; twice a year is better.

Business plan

A business plan spells out your endeavor from a business point of view in terms of how you will use your financial resources. Making a business plan is always worth your time, even if you are not applying for a loan. You never know, you might find an interested investor.

Examples of many different types of business plans are available on the Internet.

Accounting

Creative chaos can be inspiring. But if you are your own accountant, one thing is very important: order. You'll have to keep track of income and expenses. I do it like this: at the end of the month I lay out all of the receipts, bills, and income statements on an empty table. Then I make piles and assign a receipt to every account entry. You might want to get yourself a set of folders so that you can document your monthly finances for tax authorities at any time. If sorting receipts brings you close to a nervous breakdown, I suggest hiring an accounting service. Starting out, perhaps someone you know will do your monthly bookkeeping in exchange for . . . a designer handbag.

Tax filing

I recommend hiring a tax professional with whom you have a good rapport. Choose someone whom you can bombard with questions, whose answers you understand, and who advises you with an eye toward the future. Study the monthly and yearly statements, ask questions, and get a second opinion on any advice. After all, it's your business.

Type of company

In addition to planning and financing a start-up, you'll have to figure out which type of company, or legal entity, is best for you. The type of company determines how profits are calculated, what taxes are payable, and what your obligations are regarding accounting and bookkeeping. This is why you should get detailed advice from an accountant and a lawyer. Below are three options for setting up a business structure.

Sole proprietor

This is the simplest form of a business. Your profit is added to your other income and taxed. The bureaucratic hurdles are the lowest in this case. However, if you go bankrupt, both your private and business capital is at risk.

Partnership

A partnership consists of two or more people working together for the same goal, even without a written agreement. In this case, however, your personal assets are up for grabs if anything goes wrong. Keep in mind that you are liable for the decisions of your partner(s).

Limited Liability Company (LLC)

Many business owners choose to set up a limited liability company, which can be done with or without a partner. This type of entity separates the owners' personal assets from the company's liability, so it protects the owner's bank account if a judgment is brought against the business. It also has tax benefits: the owners report their share of profit and loss on their personal tax returns, rather than filing a corporate tax return.

Marketing

Image

Take steps to get your brand known from the very beginning. Present your work whenever you can and target a niche market. When you start out, you have to compensate for being unknown by being original. Try to incorporate something unique and personal into your collection. Marketing and self-promotion work best when you are authentic.

A good name

Coming up with a good label name can be challenging. Ideally, it should reflect the philosophy of your product. Make sure the name is not too trendy, because after three years it might seem dated. One solution is to use your own name. A product associated with a first and last name suggests that a person has put his or her name behind the brand. The same advice applies to the logo. Think about how it will look when it is printed or embroidered. Use a word processor to look at the many different fonts available.

Target group

Keep in mind your target market when developing your label and image. What are this group's consumer habits? This issue is often not taken seriously. There are designers who create museum-worthy pieces that only the wealthy can afford. This market segment is highly competitive and has been owned by the luxury brands for decades.

Advertising/public relations

What actions will you take to reach potential buyers? Think about your "message" and how it will draw attention. Consider placing an online ad, outfitting a celebrity, or sending an original bag to the fashion reporter of a well-known magazine. Your first customers will likely be friends and acquaintances.

Postcards and flyers

Many advertising materials are inexpensive to produce and easy to distribute at shows, parties, and in target neighborhoods. Many online shops offer low-cost printing services.

Look book

The look book, or portfolio, is a small catalog with photos of your work, and high-quality photography is important. The book is intended to educate the press, dealers, and customers about your collection. It may include a list of upcoming shows where you're exhibiting. The book can take the form of a CD or DVD, a poster or glossy printed catalog, or be as basic as a spiral-bound photo album. When you visit fairs and exhibitions, glean inspiration by asking designers whom you admire to have a look at their book.

Marketing

Product labels and tags

Boost your collection's recognition value by putting your brand name on the products. One good option is a permanent label in the form of a metal badge, a rivet with the logo, or a textile tag stamped into the leather or embroidered into the fabric. A second option is a removable tag such as a card. These cards offer convenient places for dealers to put the price tag. In addition to being attractive, they should include care instructions, material and product number, the name of your label, and your web address.

Website

Your homepage is your calling card on the web, and its design should match the color and style of your brand image. The website is often the first point of contact for customers and the press who want to find out about your business. You can hire a graphic designer or make your own website using a web-based template. Either way, consider the site's structure. The site should briefly describe who you are and what you do, and include easy-to-find contact information as well as photos of your collection. The trend is toward simple and clear sites that are updated regularly and connected to a company Facebook page and blog.

If you own a sewing machine that can do embroidery, make your label on a band of your choice. Simple!

To make your own tags, follow the business card tips. All you need is a hole punch and a nice piece of card stock. You can have them professionally made in low quantities. Use the web to find print suppliers.

Business supplies: business cards and stationery

In order to support your enterprise, you will need office supplies, including business cards, stationery, and a logo stamp. When you start out, you don't need to hire a high-end advertising agency. After all, you are creative! Do-it-yourself is the way to go.

Business cards should feature your name, company name, address, email, and website. Standard size is $3\frac{1}{2} \times 2$ inches.

Create business cards by putting your logo stamp on old filing cards, subway tickets, posters, poker playing cards, handmade paper, or whatever inspires you. Add the most important information, glue or sew them, and print.

You can use your product tag (if you already have one) as your business card by adding a sticker with your address on the back.

When you stumble upon an appealing website, jot down what you like and use it to inform your own website design.

Your stationery should match your business cards. Design the letterhead and corresponding envelopes on your computer. Word processing programs like Microsoft Word or layout software like Adobe InDesign can be used to make your letterhead. Be creative and experiment with paper quality.

Workplace

How much workspace do you need to start a business in which sewing machines, printers, a computer, office furniture, and shelves are required? You will also need storage room for fabrics, materials, and finished products. For ideas, check out the workspaces of colleagues and apprentices in the fashion industry.

Working from home

Working from home is inexpensive. If you go this route, try to set up a dedicated room for work. This eliminates distractions, as working from home requires a lot of discipline. A restaurant or quiet coffee shop is the best place to meet with business partners and customers.

Shared workshop

When you have your own office, you can rattle away with the sewing machine and turn up the music without disturbing anyone. Conversations about prices, quantities, and contracts remain private. However, you will also be isolated. With a shared workshop you can share fixed costs such as rent, utilities, Internet, printer, and kitchen and save a lot of money. Furthermore, chatting among colleagues can be motivating—in the best case, it creates synergy. I recommend sharing space with graphic designers or computer specialists, but being close to other fashion designers can be inspiring, too. At the end of the day it is important that the chemistry is right, because you will probably spend more time with your studio partners than you will with your loved ones.

Workshop with retail shop

The advantage here is that you can sell directly and get feedback from customers. You also have an additional source of income to cover some of the costs. However, this set-up involves more paperwork.

As you start out, try to keep your investments and fixed costs low; used shelves, sewing machines, computers, and tables are good enough and many times their cost is only half of new items.

Negotiate the rent; sometimes there is wiggle room. Pay attention to cancellation periods, mandatory renovations, and additional expenses.

Production

Where should you get your creations manufactured? It is not easy to find a manufacturer who will make your product with the desired quality and volume at a fair price. Plan carefully so that you can compete with larger businesses. Quality, price, and volume are significant challenges, even for large fashion companies.

In-house production

When you are just starting out, producing on your own is the safest method to assure quality and turn out small quantities. This, of course, requires that you are trained and have the required machines. Be sure to factor in your salary when calculating the price of your product.

Outsourcing locally

Consider outsourcing production to well-trained professionals who work from home. If you live nearby, you can keep an eye on them. This will give you the opportunity to get small quantities produced while you take care of other aspects of your business.

Workshop subcontractors

Subcontractors manufacture small quantities of items. As with the options mentioned above, you are responsible for supplying the materials.

Full-service production facilities

These suppliers are able to make a prototype from real material when you provide a detailed design sketch—that is, they deliver patterns and prototypes and organize the material purchases. Many of these companies are located abroad, so the production is often cheaper but fraught with many problems.

Communication, customs, shipping, and long delivery time often hamper fluid collaboration. Take into account that the delivery may take several months and that you risk receiving your product late. This production method works for producing quantities in the hundreds. Do your homework. When you find a promising supplier, invest in an airline ticket to get a first-hand impression of your production partner.

Price calculation

There are different methods of calculating prices for products. A basic rule is to add 30 to 40 percent to the manufacturing cost. But you should certainly make a detailed cost analysis. Some products are cheaper to produce, so you might want to use different percentages with different models. Also, purchasers will like the fact that they can get a good entry price for one or two models in your collection. If you sell to retailers, keep in mind their price calculation, too. Many retailers multiply the purchase price by three. You also need to compare the quality of your product with the calculated price. Does the $300 bag look like it is worth $300? You can lower your costs if you manufacture a model in large quantities, or if you use a base design for all your bags.

Sales

Your workplace is furnished, you created the name for your label, the sample collection has been produced, and you have calculated the prices. Now the most important part of the job lies ahead: sales.

Invest as much diligence into your sales strategy as you did on your designs. As beautiful as your bags may be, they won't sell by themselves. There are numerous ways of selling, from the cost-effective online shop to an elaborate booth at trade shows. Following are some typical sales options. But beware: if you don't have many years of experience and contacts, start small. Keep your initial investment as low as possible and let it grow with your business. Of course, creating a professional image, producing your collection, marketing . . . all this costs money. It may take several seasons for your investments to pay off. You need a long breath—it may take at least three years.

Fortunately, bags are not vulnerable to seasonal fashion trends. Designers often change only colors and minor details to maintain their recognition value.

Retail sales

The advantage here is that retailers take care of the product's presentation and sales. The disadvantage is that many retailers only work on commission, so you need to keep track of which and how many items you deliver.

Always keep a written record of your deliveries. Provide your sales conditions and transaction rules and quote the gross and net price on your invoice.

Note that different tax rules may apply when you sell to foreign countries.

Production and sales timing

Here is an elaborate but low-cost method for getting your products into stores. Look for boutiques and stores where your product would be well-represented. Act professionally: get an appointment with the buyer and send a catalog and a price list before the meeting. Generally, there are two sales windows in a given year: the fall/winter season and the spring/summer season; dealers order six months before the season. This means that the collection has to be developed a year before it gets into the stores.

Sales

Trade fairs

Research the appropriate fairs for your collection. For example, where does your competition exhibit its products? Talk to designers who have attended fairs. Identify boutiques where you want to sell your collection and send them invitations to the trade fair.

Ask trade fair organizers whether they offer entry discounts for emerging designers. Sometimes subsidies are available.

Distributing agencies and agents

If you are an unknown brand, it might not be easy to find an enthusiastic distributor; however, the fashion industry is always on the lookout for the next new thing. Agencies have deep market experience and purchasing contacts. Agencies usually charge a sales commission of 10–15%.

Direct sales

The advantage here is that you receive the full margin of the sold product, but you will have to invest a lot of time on adverising, sales, shipping, and dealing with complaints.

Your own store

With your own store you have the closest contact with customers. If your store is also your workshop, you have an opportunity to satisfy the wishes of individual customers.

Online shop

Handbags do not involve the terror of size and fit, so online sales are a good option. Nowadays it is not difficult to set up an online shop. The Internet offers many templates for this purpose. However, you should also invest in marketing (with Google, Facebook, Twitter, and newsletters) to attract customers to your shop. If this is too much trouble for you, consider joining successful online shops such as Etsy.

Markets for young designers

Large cities, in particular, offer more and more markets and fairs for young designers. They offer the participants an affordable platform to present themselves, make contacts with purchasers and customers, exchange opinions and ideas with like-minded design colleagues, and most importantly, to sell the products directly.